INSTAGR.

Beginners Guide for Instagram Influencers

(The Playbook for Increasing Your Following and Generating Profits)

Michael Bradford

Published by Andrew Zen

Michael Bradford

All Rights Reserved

Instagram: Beginners Guide for Instagram Influencers (The Playbook for Increasing Your Following and Generating Profits)

ISBN 978-1-989965-80-1

Legal & Disclaimer

The information contained in this book is not designed to replace or take the place of any form of medicine or professional medical advice. The information in this book has been provided for educational and entertainment purposes only.

The information contained in this book has been compiled from sources deemed reliable, and it is accurate to the best of the Author's knowledge; however, the Author cannot guarantee its accuracy and validity and cannot be held liable for any errors or omissions. Changes are periodically made to this book. You must consult your doctor or get professional medical advice before using any of the suggested remedies, techniques, or information in this book.

Upon using the information contained in this book, you agree to hold harmless the Author from and against any damages, costs, and expenses, including any legal fees potentially resulting from the application of any of the information provided by this guide. This disclaimer applies to any damages or injury caused by the use and application, whether directly or indirectly, of any advice or information presented, whether for breach of contract, tort, negligence, personal injury, criminal intent, or under any other cause of action.

You agree to accept all risks of using the information presented inside this book. You need to consult a professional medical practitioner in order to ensure you are both able and healthy enough to participate in this program.

Table of Contents

Introduction

2018 was a banner year for Instagram with more marketers turning to the service than ever before. While this influx of interest has brought new lifeblood to the service, it has also seen some new changes which means you will need to be aware of the latest and greatest if you want to continue to see results. The following list of trends is sure to shape the future of Instagram marketing from 2020 onwards.

Vertical Video

If you are still looking for proof that all trends reverse if given enough time, look no further than the reemergence of vertical video. While this was once a clear sign that the person who took the video didn't quite know what they were doing, it is now a burgeoning Instagram trend that is sure only to continue blowing up in the coming year. Vertical video is also becoming more acceptable on other sites including Vimeo and YouTube. All this makes it clear that vertical video is not going away which means now is the time to learn to create and edit them properly in order to ensure that you are ready to capitalize on this trend for as long as possible.

If you haven't yet, then now is the time to learn basic video editing skills, even if you commonly work with a video team as it is always a good idea to understand how to edit down a longer video for an Instagram story. To add extra production value to your Instagram stories, consider secondary apps like Storeo or Inshot. There are a few choices when it comes to creating an acceptable vertical video, and you can actually trim down video shot horizontally so it looks as though you were savvy enough to hop on this latest retro trend.

It is important to keep in mind, however, that there is a big difference between natively filming in vertical mode and cropping things later and simply hoping it all works out in the end. The most important aspects of the shot that you need to plan for when it comes to vertical video is that everyone remains clearly recognizable which means not cutting off the heads of anyone in the shot and ensuring that you don't end up cutting out any of the good stuff in the process. Current trends suggest that many people feel as though this type of content is actually more engaging than the alternative which means your marketing efforts will see more views and people will consume longer chunks of the content as a whole.

While shooting proper vertical video is relatively straightforward, editing it can be more difficult than you might expect. If you have already edited video then it is certainly within your wheelhouse, it will just take some practice in order to get things down pat. There are a few ways to go about doing so, starting with editing the content on your phone directly.

If you are using an iPhone, then you won't be able to edit vertical video in iMovie which means you will need to go with a third-party app such as Bolt or InShot which will allow you to create vertical videos that still display in 16:9. If you have some more time or want to do something extra special with your video, then you may want to switch to using iMovie on your laptop or computer instead. This is a must if you are interested in adding various layers to your video or things like graphics or text. Doing so will require you to rotate your video clips after editing and then flip them in QuickTime after they have been exported, but these steps are easy to manage after the first few tries.

Even still, if you are planning on creating a lot of intricate video content, then you are likely better off taking the plunge and going the professional software route with something like Adobe Premiere Pro. While this tier of software requires a fair bit of tutorial before it can be used easily, the end result will be superior every single time.

Instagram Stories with AR Filters

A major theme of the 2018 F8 Facebook conference was how augmented reality and virtual reality are going to be influencing social media sooner than the public might expect and one such way in which they are future-proofing their services is by offering more and more augmented reality filters as time goes by.

Getting in on these options and becoming comfortable with them as soon as possible is sure to pay dividends in the future.

Not only are the face filters that Instagram offers a forward-thinking example of how AR can be used in traditional scenarios, brands, influencers and creators of all types can also create their very own unique variations on these options through the use of Facebook's AR studio. While only a few major brands like Kylie Jenner and Rihanna have used this option so far, you can expect to see more and more similar entities taking advantage of this option in the years to come. What makes these filters so useful from a social media perspective is that they are only available to those who follow the women on Instagram, which means it not only ensures their current fans feel special, it also gives those on the fence a reason to join up that is advertised, for free, every time an existing follower uses the filter.

Many filters often give viewers the opportunity to try out a filter that their friends are using which means that AR Filters on Instagram stories are literally created to go viral right from the very start so expect to see a lot of growth in this area in the next year.

Offline Events

As surprising as it might sound, 2019 may very well see the return of the physical meetup thanks to an emerging trend of Instagram taking key influencers on vacation to specific locations. While this is certainly an expensive option, it is certainly a guaranteed way to generate a large number of likes and to sell a large number of products in the process. Companies like Boohoo, Benefit and Revolve are already seeing results taking a small group of highly curated influencers on vacation to take advantage of their existing followings. What they are doing is essentially forcing the illusion of the "cool" lifestyle by inviting viewers to follow along every step of the way and buy all of the cool things they see. Outside of this new example of influencer marketing, another new trend that is really starting to take off is curated museums of the "perfect" Instagram picture.

The real future, however, lies with brands like Refinery 29 Rooms which blend real-world exhibitions with curated experiences, giving participants plenty of opportunities to interact with the brand in a positive way and also post about it in a way that is sure to get plenty of likes on social media. While creating an offline experience can be a lot of work, it can be an excellent way to gain lots of followers quickly while also generating sales at the same time. It is essentially word of mouth for the modern age. When a customer has a positive experience that is also worthy of an Instagram post then it is far more likely to end up on their page where all of their friends can see and interact with it themselves.

The cocktail bar Her Majesty's Pleasure in Toronto is a perfect example of a business that took this idea to heart. While boasting a reasonable amount of business most of the time, by simply updating their theme and décor to more directly appeal to women between the ages of 25 and 34, they managed to grow their followers by more than 26,000 a serious accomplishment for a small local bar. The beauty of this approach is that you don't need an existing physical location in order to create Instagram experiences, you can simply team up with existing like-minded businesses and ensure that everyone benefits from the added exposure.

Instagram Shopping

Throughout 2018 Instagram has been releasing and retooling its shopping features, but they are stable enough now that you can expect to see serious traction in this area in 2020 and beyond. Beyond simply tagging products in specific posts, users now have the ability to tag stories to specific products thanks to the new shopping tab that can be found on the Explore page. Rumor has it that soon brands will be able to link up with influencers directly from within the app and that these influencers will be able to tag specific brands as well as products in their posts.

There are a variety of different ways to make sales from Instagram, each of which will ultimately work better with some segments of the market than others. What works for your target audience may surprise you which is why it is best to try as many different approaches as possible as you never know when you will land on a gold mine. Getting started now will allow you to head into 2020 with a new and improved strategy ready to go.

Ads in Instagram Stories

As popular as they have become, it was only a matter of time before Story specific ads started popping up and 2020 will be the year that they explode in a big way. Current estimates suggest that around 400 million people watch Instagram Stories each and every day which is ideal because it currently offers a far greater return on investment than a similar Facebook ad due to the reduced costs and comparable reach in some scenarios.

As this is still a young form of advertising, it is important to take as full advantage of it as you can before the price increases to accurately reflect its usefulness. This is the perfect time to try out a variety of different formats for your ads to ensure that your game is on point by the time even more people start paying attention. Rather than cropping an existing photo or creating something entirely new, when it comes to ads for specific stories you can still get away with just adding a top and bottom banner in relevant colors. Taking the time to include mentions, emojis, and texts in the ads will help them look more natural as well.

When considering these types of ads, it is important to keep in mind that when people tune in to Instagram Stories they expect to see casual content as opposed to things that are more highly produced which means you will want your ad to have the same aesthetic in order to ensure that people don't immediately swipe past it. Keywords here should be organic and filter-less videos.

Chapter 1: The Instagram World

Since 2010, Instagram has been proven to be the fastest-growing social media platform. But what makes this platform unique and effective? Well, what separates it from the rest is the creativity it offers.

Instagram has generated creative ways for users to share their content. For example, Instagram has allowed its users to share 10-second videos or photos on their account that disappears after 24 hours, it's meant to rival Snapchat and apparently, they won as more people prefer using it now rather than the original creator of the concept. The platform also allows users to show live videos that allow users to have real-time interactions with their followers – IG Live.

So, basically, their tactics just seem to always work and it gives so much advantage to people who want to market their business. The innovation it offers is one of the main reasons for its sudden, continuous boom.

Is it worth the fuss?

Instagram is the perfect app for sharing content via visual imagery. Generally, its audience is young, educated, and very into shopping. It has a different feel compared to platforms like Facebook and Twitter, with a focus on visuals rather than words. However, studies have shown that, like Facebook, it is used daily and makes for a loyal and highly active user base.

This ability to capture a younger, more creative audience is sounding the alarm bells for major companies who are looking to advertise on social media. With high usage, the increased interest in advertising on the app is not surprising. However, the competition is extreme so businesses will have to find creative ways to compete with their rivals in this visual haven of social media.

1.1 Knowing the Crowd of Instagram

Keeping yourself aware of Instagram's demographic is important in order for you to determine how you would get around in using this platform to your business' full advantage. This is important because by getting yourself familiar with the number, you will be able to plan your tactics better. This will prevent you from wasting your time creating content that will not work for the types of followers you might not have.

What you want is to invest your time in is presenting the applicable content for the right audience. On Instagram, because you are mostly using images and videos as the main content, you need to create images and graphics that are appropriate and captive to your following base. A great content strategy equals to good engagement.

Instagram demographics by age and gender

While there's still no way to know the specific demographics of your own followers, you may still want to know the general demographics of the entire platforms. Unsurprisingly, Instagram leans towards a much younger audience.

Here is the demographic for Instagram users:

13-17-year-olds – 72%

18-29-year-olds – 64%

30-49-year-olds – 40%

50-64-year-olds – 21%

65+-year-olds – 10%

Instagram demographics by gender

When it comes to gender, Instagram is more popular among females than males, but the difference is not that drastic. It shows that 50.3% of Instagram users are female, while the remaining 49.7% are male.

Instagram demographics by location

Although Instagram is available all over the world – except China, Iran, and North Korea – there are some countries that spend more time on it than the others.

A great way to manage your digital marketing strategy is to look at the statistics that show the usage of your target countries. When you know which countries use Instagram most, it's going to be easier for you to adapt and customize your content based on the audience going to be exposed to it.

With about 700 million monthly active users, the United States ranks number one when it comes to having the highest number of Instagram users and it's not really surprising.

However, despite having the largest Instagram active users, the United States has only a 34% penetration rate, which is lower compared to the highest penetration rate country, Aruba with a rate of 46% despite having only 4.7 million active users.

More than 80% of people who use Instagram are based outside the US, with some of the top countries including India, Brazil, India, and different countries in Europe.

Now, let's breakdown these users by region:

users from urban areas – 42%

users from suburban areas – 34%

users from rural areas – 25%

How Fast Instagram is Growing

Instagram picks up new accounts faster than ever – especially since the app allows users to sign in up to 5 accounts in a single device. This gives users the ability to run their personal Instagram account along with their Instagram business accounts using a single phone.

As of this year, the platform gets about 1 billion monthly active users. And this number makes them the third most

popular social media platform today –
following Facebook with 2 billion monthly
users and YouTube with 1.9 monthly
active users.

The number of monthly active users is a
commonly used metric with some sort of
limitation. The figure doesn't allow for
much nuance: a person who scrolls and
posts to Instagram multiple times a day
is way more important to the service than
those who check in every once in a while.
And growth for a certain period may
include returning lapsed users, although
that's not really that important.

Caveats aside, these numbers are
definitely impressive. According to
Instagram, the factors behind
this continuous growth has something to
do with its smart algorithm that allows
users to easily find their interests easily.
On top of it, the constant updates that add
new features and improves the old
ones make so much difference.

Chapter 2: Growing Your Brand With Instagram

Why is Instagram so valuable for your brand?

Instagram is a very powerful tool for marketing businesses. It provides a medium for organic advertising and allows you to engage directly with your target audience. It also provides tools that make advertising easier for businesses. These tools reduce the number of links or processes a potential buyer has to go through before making a purchase, making it easier for users to find you and buy from you.

Let's go through the steps that will help you get a massive boost in your business using Instagram.

Things to avoid at all costs

First, we will take a look at the things you might be doing wrong and you should avoid at all costs.

You may be wondering why you are not generating sales through Instagram, read the following points and analyze if any of them resonate with what you are doing:

1.   The Spammy Sam: A lot of businesses make this mistake. They make all the posts about their services, products, and how wonderful they are, without telling their audience how this product or service will help them out. There are lots of other businesses doing exactly what you do. The only reason a potential buyer will want to buy your product or service is because it solves a problem for them. There's absolutely no way they will know you can solve this problem if you don't let them know. SELL, SELL, SELL is a NO, NO, NO. In other words, create content that will help your audience solve their problems, let them know how you can

help make their lives easier and the sales will come to you.

2.	The Scared Tom: This type of user or brand doesn't bother to use their content to convert the follower into a buyer. The prospect buyer can't relate your content to the problem they are facing. Hence, they ignore all the posts you make and move on to other sellers. Align your content to the problems your audience is facing, and communicate in a similar language your audience uses. What are their pain points? What makes you different from your competition? Are you posting often? Don't be scared to tell people why you are awesome and why they should use you above the competition! But always remember, don't focus on selling, focus on solving problems for your followers.

What will attract buyers to you

People need solutions to the challenges they are facing. Since you have a solution to this problem, it is your job to find those that need this solution. For you to attract buyers that will stick with your brand, and will be loyal, you have to offer value and then build trust.

Now, some of the mistakes that may be preventing you from making profit through Instagram have been noted. Let's move on to the next step which is setting up your Instagram account correctly.

Setting up your account correctly

Selling with Instagram starts with setting up your account correctly.

Steps to take when setting up your account:

While signing up, ensure you verify your mobile number. This is important for security reasons.

When a buyer is trying to find your business, the first thing they will search for is your name. The main thing that will set you apart from other businesses is picking a name and profile picture that will make your buyer remember your brand always.

When writing your bio, you have to make it 100% about your target audience. You have to share with your audience why they need to do business with you and how you are going to help them. Remember, you have to keep it simple and to the point.   Add a description that will provide a summary of what your business does.

Include a link to your landing page. You can also include a video, link to download eBook, or any lead magnet method y ou have available. If you don't have a lead magnet, you can still send them to your blog or   SITE . The main goal here is to provide a means of giving your audience value. Instagram doesn't allow its users to post so many links, you just have one slot for a link. Therefore, ensure that whatever link you are putting   is relevant to your business. Instagram is just a point of contact with your audience, where do you want them to go next? To your SHOPIFY STORE ? To get more info about you? To send an email? Directing the online traffic you are getting from your social media account will add credibility to your business.

Add your profile picture. Adding pictures helps to increase credibility. It helps to build a relationship between you and followers. Do not be tempted to use a selfie. If you want to be treated like a professional, you have to act that way. A professional headshot is recommended to be used.

From time to time, you can view your profile from a follower's point of view. It will help you know if you are moving in the right direction. When you click on the right button or tap on your profile page, you will be able to see the engagement options that your followers will see when they take a look at your business profile.

Chapter 3: Instagram

What is it?

Instagram is a very popular smartphone social media platform.

This app allows you to post endless pictures and videos and view other people from all over the world.

It is a way to document your everyday life through photos and share them with your followers or select groups of friends.

You can see comments or send posts found on Instagram.

In April 2002, Facebook, a social network giant, acquired the application for approximately US$1 billion in cash and stocks.

A number of changes have been made to the application that make it more similar to the Facebook app.

This progress is believed to have contributed to the success which it enjoys today.

We live in a visual age, in which people are moved by what they see.

That is why companies spend so much money on publicity campaigns on posters, billboards, and TV advertising.

A product is bound to have a stronger impression on someone if it is visually pleasant or intriguing.

Most Instagram users are located in countries outside the USA.

This means that companies will have free access to a global audience.

Installing Instagram and building a blog are free of charge, which is a big benefit for companies.

They have now taken advantage of the marketing opportunity provided by the application.

This is because the use of social media has enabled them to reach potential customers without spending large amounts of money.

Features of Instagram

Instagram Questions—This feature was introduced recently in July 2018 and allows Instagram users to answer questions posted by their followers.

Although the answers to questions are not anonymous, you can post them to your story, and the name of the questioner is anonymous.

This feature is very popular among users.

Instagram Direct—Direct allows you to share photos, videos, hashtag pages, profiles, and locations directly from your news feed with a single person or a small group of people. You can access your inbox at the top right of the feed page from the inbox icon.

Instagram Stories—Stories allow users to post a picture/video selection in one story.

This relatively new feature works much like Snapchat stories, and after 24 hours, your story will disappear.

They are not posted on the profile or news feed of the user. Instagram stories allow the same configuration of privacy as Instagram users.

For example, if the user has a private account and posts a story, the story can only be viewed by user friends.

When was it created?

It was released as an app in fall 2010 and has flourished immensely, since then, it has become one of today's most popular social media platforms.

It was made by Mike Krieger and Kevin Systrom.

Since 2010, the app has been updated on numerous occasions, so it has completely changed and is nothing like the Instagram we used 8 years ago.

The app is free for everyone around the world

How do you use it?

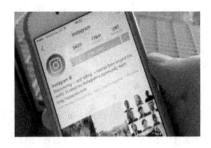

It is used daily to share photos and videos, watch Instagram TV, and stream live.

You create an account, and from there, you can explore all the tools it offers, including a story that you can add to every day, tags that you can look up, and even private messaging like Facebook.

Once you create an account, the app shows you exactly how to navigate your Instagram account, which should allow you to use the app with little to no questions about how to use the app.

Instagram can also be used to manage a business account; the app has recently released a ton of new business tools that are ideal for business accounts.

There are such things as shoppable Instagram posts that direct you to online shopping via the app itself.

You can also attach links in stories that make it easy to expand your business and/or buyers on site.

What are the benefits?

This app allows you to keep your friends and family up to date on your life through pictures and videos, vice versa.

Allows you to keep in touch with people you have relationships with.

Is a way to promote positive feedback on people and lifestyles, and to receive positive feedback on your own.

Can be used to promote your business, giving people access to web pages, emails, and information pertaining to your business.

Can be used to gather information on a place or person, especially if they are a celebrity or a musician.

Used to make friends and introduce people to new places and other people.

Used to grow a fan base, otherwise described as a social group that you interact emotionally but not physically with.

What are the risks?

A risk of using Instagram is that you could be cyberbullied by someone, often people like to use Instagram in negative ways.

If you experience unnecessary hate or harassment online, always screenshot the messages and block/report the antagonizer.

Often used to promote pornography/violent things that kids should not be viewing.

If you are a parent, you can set up parental controls, disabling your child from seeing such things. Report illegal content!

When you first sign up, your profile is automatically public, making it so that anyone using the app can see your profile.

You usually want to make your account private to avoid anything suspicious.

Can be dangerous if you don't protect your account and password. Hackers do exist in the world and could access your personal information from Instagram.

Allows inappropriate or dangerous conversations to go on because anyone can private message anyone. The app has recently made it so that you have to accept incoming messages from people not following you.

Building a Strong Instagram Profile

The perfect Instagram name

— Choosing the perfect name of Instagram can be crucial for your blog.

The name must be simple and preferably similar to your Instagram's focus.

People need to recognize you directly and easily.

This means that your name has to be recognizable and must appear immediately during a search.

When you think about different usernames you can use, you need to design them in a way that inspires a good idea about your focus for your followers.

Remember that you are not an internationally renowned brand or celebrity right off the bat.

You create a new profile, and you need to work on getting followers.

If you use a nondescript username or something equally obscure, people won't be as aware of you as they want them to be.

Before you decide on a username for your profile, it is a good idea to learn about all those users and businesses that do not grow on Instagram before starting.

This usually happens when people become disappointed or even confused when they realize that the Instagram content does not match the name.

If you have trouble coming up with a name, try to ask family members or someone you trust to give you a legitimate answer.

Maybe even ask some people on Instagram or give them some of your own suggestions.

Their honest response and feedback should help you to choose the perfect name.

Your name should have these qualities:

Easy to pronounce so that people can repeat it easily without having to write it down.

Unique because no two usernames can be the same, you don't want to end up copying someone else's.

Periods and underscores; that is if you need to use them.

Make sure they are organized within your username, so it doesn't look out of place at all.

Needs to be short. If you have to long of a username, it will most likely not be easy to pronounce.

Should avoid gender, ethnic, or religion biased names. This can cause a specific group of people to dislike your blog, and you do not want that.

Avoid common names if you use a super common name that will eliminate the uniqueness of your username.

The logo

—You may already have written and implemented a social media marketing campaign for your brand, but you need to make sure you have a logo.

It is quintessential for your brand and is critical for any marketing strategy.

If your brand has a logo, people will always associate your company with it whenever they see it.

A logo is an important part of branding, especially if you want to use social media to market your company online.

You need to consider many aspects to create the perfect logo, including the font, tagline, designs, colors, and more.

When you design a social media logo, you need to take into account a few different variables. Your work doesn't end there, even if you create the perfect logo.

When designing the logo, separate text and graphics are recommended.

You must ensure that the text and the graphics you are using are different components of the logo.

This is useful if you have to convert your logo to a different size.

In fact, many brands and companies tend to use a single social media letter or graphic to facilitate their conversion. Keep in mind simplicity when designing your logo.

You can add your logo to your photos or add it to your social media platforms as a watermark.

You can even use it as a profile picture on Instagram.

By doing so, your customers form a perception of your brand that will remain forever with them.

Your logo will help you by:

Promoting your business

Creating an identity for your brand

Showing your viewers professionalism

Giving followers a look into who and what you are

Instagram bio

—You need to understand the different components that compromise your Instagram bio.

Once you have done so, you can add more details to improve your account so that users understand what your brand is all about and what they can expect when they follow you.

The main problem you face when you compose a bio is the relatively small amount of space you have.

The bio section on Instagram only allows 150 characters, and your username must fit under 30 characters. With more than 800 million users active in the app, you must optimize your chances of being discovered and pursue an effective marketing approach.

The bio must be concise and captivating to make an impression.

A catchy bio can attract people to follow you and encourage them to work with you.

If your main goal is Instagram marketing, make sure you have a killer bio.

Here are some ways to make your bio brilliant:

Include a tagline

Be minimalistic

Link your other accounts

Use a branded hashtag

Make use of emoji

Use link breaks

Include your contact information

Say a little something about what makes you unique as an individual

Profile picture

—You want to make sure that it draws people who visit your profile for the first time when you choose a profile picture. Your profile picture is seen by your followers all over Instagram.

You see it almost everywhere.

If you have a business profile, you want to make your profile picture something that is related to your company. Generally, you want your picture to represent what your blog is about.

It doesn't have to be a photo of you, get creative!

Use Stories

—If you want to share your experiences with all your Instagram followers, use Instagram Stories.

It's better than uploading an image and offers a few different options to spice up your photos or videos. Instagram stories are very similar to Instagram's feed, but the difference between the two is that the first one is more visual.

This feature lets you post your photo or video in the Stories section and not upload it as normal.

You can share the stories you create on Instagram with a group of people or even with a single user.

Once you post a story, it's available 24 hours before it's gone. It's pretty similar to the Snapchat story.

Instagram has recently added an update called Highlights, where you can pin stories previously posted to your profile, allowing users to see what you put on your story every time they click on a highlight.

Instagram Stories is an excellent way to increase your statistics. Although this is a popular feature, many users do not know how to correctly use the feature.

If you do not make good use of it, you cannot reap all the benefits that it has to offer.

One good thing about this feature is that it's simple, and you learn all you need to know when you create a profile.

Here are some ways Instagram Stories can help you:

It can generate curiosity, drawing people to your profile.

It can give people more of an insight into your everyday life without being annoying.

You can use this feature to tag friends and introduce followers to other followers.

You can create some really cool stuff from the filters and live filters it offers.

Chapter 4: Laying The Groundwork

"You have to learn the rules of the game. And then you have to play better than anyone else." – Albert Einstein.

In order to succeed on Instagram we need to understand the basics of the environment we have to work with. Take your time reading the following sections to understand the basic rules of Instagram. In the most straightforward way, there are two variables we have to understand — the first is Instagram's famous Algorithm. The second variable are Instagram Users.

How The Algorithm Works

"... We build systems that try to understand who and what you ... care about, and use that information to help you create, find, join, and share in experiences that matter to you ... and offering ways for you to experience

45

Instagram based on things you ... do on and off Instagram." – Instagram

At first glance, it seems like everything that Instagram does is showing you the content of people and companies you care about and love. Even though Instagram is free for everyone to use, they are a business — and being a business means earning money.

We will look at how we can use the knowledge we acquire in this section for our advantage later in the book.

Remember: Maximizing their income is what Instagram, next to other things, is trying to do. Therefore, earning money will be a thriving factor in how the Algorithm operates.

Attention: Nobody outside Instagram knows if the following information is accurate. You can be pretty sure though that the information presented below is close to the truth.

Instagram's Business Model

The primary income source for Instagram is selling ad-space. Some posts and stories you encounter on the App are advertisements. Presenting more sponsored posts to users equals more income for Instagram. The Algorithm is only able to display a certain number of ads to a user in a specific timeframe so that the user enjoys the experience on Instagram. The only way to get more opportunities to present advertisements is users that stay online longer.

Engaged users are more likely to click on an advertisement. If a user clicks on an ad, the marketer who paid for the ad sees results from his marketing campaign. The more clicks the marketer gets, the higher the likelihood that the marketer will purchase another campaign. The only way to increase the number of clicks on advertisements is to present users' content they will engage with because they enjoy it.

Remember: The more users are online and the longer a user is online, the more potential for the Algorithm to present advertisements. Engaged users are more likely to click on an ad resulting in more ad campaigns. Because of that, the Algorithm will try to keep users online and engaged as long as possible.

Homework: Open your Instagram app, scroll through your feed, and count the frequency of advertisements on your feed. At the time of writing this book, Instagram presents an ad on every fifth post. Also, check if the content of the ads is relevant to you.

How the Algorithm works

The only way to keep someone doing what they are doing is if they enjoy it. Instagram's Algorithm is machine-based learning. It learns what you like and care about as well as what you don't like. The Algorithm uses three signals to determine if you want to see particular content or not.

Interest

Instagram predicts how much you will enjoy a post determined by your past behaviour. To do so, the Algorithm looks at the content you interacted with in the past. It analyses these posts looking at hashtags, post descriptions, even vision analysing the image or video. After examining these things, Instagram identifies, amongst other things, what subjects you are interested in, what colours you prefer, and what kind of descriptions you would like to read. Based on all that information, the Algorithm decides what content it will present to you in the future.

Recency

Newer posts show up at the top.

Relationship

Instagram identifies how close you are to other users. Let's say you are following two users, Julia and Christoph. You always engage with Julia's content. You watch her stories, like her images, and chat with her. On the other hand, you don't look at Christoph's content. Based on that observation, Instagram will know that you are closer to Julia than you are to Christoph. Because of that, the Algorithm presents Julia's content in front of Christoph's content.

Homework: Go to your feed, look at your stories, and look at the first five accounts. Do you like watching their stories? Are they funny, motivating, or useful? **Remember:** To maximize the time you spend online and to make you engage, Instagram has to show you content that matters to you. To do that, Instagram uses three ranking signals. What kind of content you see in your feed, the discover page, and individual hashtag pages depends on not one but all three ranking signals.

What the Algorithm likes

Based on what you have learned in the previous sections, you can conclude that the Algorithm likes if your content engages users and keeps them interested. Let's go through the three ranking signals and talk specifically about what Instagram likes to see.

Interest

Using the following two approaches, Instagram decides if people enjoy your content.

Time spent on your content: The more time a user spends on your post or story, the better, if ten seconds are good, twenty seconds, are better.

Insider: If a user spends a lot of time looking at your content, Instagram assumes that this particular user will come back to view your latest content. The Algorithm loves that because users coming online to see your content means more opportunity to squeeze in advertisements and earn money.

Interactions with your content and your account:

Interactions with your content can be anything from liking, commenting, direct messaging, watching a video, swiping through a carousel, watching and rewatching one of your stories, visiting your feed to share your content with others. The more interactions you get, the better.

Remember: Not every interaction is valued equally. Commenting is better than liking, rewatching a story is better than watching it the first time.

Pro Tip: Time spent on your content right after publishing, as well as interactions with your content right after publishing are more valuable than if these things happen one hour after publishing. **Remember:** Instagram doesn't care about how many followers you have. The

Algorithm cares about how many quality interactions you have with users on the Platform.

Recency and Timeliness

Two points contribute to this ranking signal. The first one doesn't have anything to do with the Algorithm per se, but it is still an important point to discuss.

The more you post, the better: Publishing more content is better, as long as you are not annoying your followers or making the Algorithm think you are spamming. More content is better because more posts mean more opportunities for users to discover your content from all around the world.

Insider: If you target people in New York at 10:00 am, you likely won't reach new users in Sydney where it's 2:00 am.

Instagram's latest features: Instagram is continuously implementing new features. Once a new feature is released, Instagram wants its users to adopt them fast. To make that happen, Instagram rewards users by giving them more reach if they use the latest features. **Homework:** If not jet enabled, allow Instagram to send you emails about new features. You may also follow Instagram's official business account on Instagram and Twitter. In addition to that, make sure to check out https://help.instagram.com for explanations on how to use Instagram's features.

Relationships

Instagram is a social network. Having organic interactions with other users in your niche indicates that you are a valuable player in your niche.

Remember: If the Algorithm recognizes that users like what you do on the Platform, it will present your content to more users who will likely also enjoy what you do. If those users again like what you do on the Platform, the Algorithm will increase your reach and present your content to more users.

What the Algorithm hates

Regulated in the community guidelines, are two things the Algorithm doesn't like. The first thing is having artificial interactions, the second one is publishing family-unfriendly content.

Artificial Interactions

Instagram doesn't like to see automated, unnatural interactions, like spamming, automatic liking bots, commenting bots, direct messaging bots, or follow bots. Insider: Automated interactions on Instagram, for example, fake the effectiveness of running advertisements on the Platform. If you want to promote your product or service to 1000 users whereof 500 users are fake, you pay for 1000 views but only get 500. Automated interactions hurt advertisers and therefore Instagram.

Family-unfriendly content

Instagram is a diverse community of cultures, ages and beliefs. Keeping every user safe while keeping Instagram an open environment for everyone requires some constraints. Instagram doesn't tolerate nudity, self-injury or unrespectful content, not even if you want to spread awareness. Users also have the opportunity to report content or actions you take on the Platform. After reporting Instagram staff will check if you violated the community guidelines. Reasons for a legit report might be sharing content that you are not allowed to publish or repeatedly contacting people for commercial purposes without their consent. **Remember:** Violating the community guidelines may result in deleted content, a disabled account or other restrictions.

Our data driven world

The Algorithm collects many data points when you do something on the Platform. You might not know that Instagram collects so-called "metadata". Amongst other things, metadata includes your location, time posted, data of your device, post description or comment content and even vision analysing your content. We already talked about Instagram's capability of vision, analysing your content. Vision-analysing is based on machine and deep learning, meaning that the Algorithm can see what is in your images or videos. If there is a shoe inside your image, Instagram will know. If you have Mount Everest in your background, Instagram will know your location even if location services are turned off. If you take a selfie with your shiny new Tesla in the frame, Instagram would be able to present advertisements to you offering the latest aftermarket parts for your new car. (Instagram is not quite there though).

Homework: If you have some coding experience or are curious, you can visit Instagram on your computer. Find one of your image posts, right-click the image klick 'inspect' and find the element inside the highlighted element. Look at the alt attribute. Did you tell Instagram that those things are in the image? I doubt.

Homework: Open your Instagram app, search for a Hashtag of your choice and look at the first posts at the top posts section. Can you make up similarities between pictures? Are there two, three, maybe four similar types of posts with similar colours and or content? Here is the best part. Take screenshots of four pictures that look similar. Put them all into an image editing tool next to each other and start blurring them more and more.

Insider: Instagram's database connects to the database of Facebook and WhatsApp. If you have connected your accounts, the Algorithm will use data from these other platforms too. As you can see, you could potentially support or hurt your Instagram presence with your Facebook or WhatsApp presence.

Understanding Instagram Users

"Whoever understands the customer best, wins." — Mike Gospe

Instagram is a global community with users from all over the world. Despite all their differences, living in different cultures, grown up in different generations, having different lifestyles, some rich some poor they all meet in one place — Instagram. To blow up your Instagram, you need to understand why and how people use the Platform. There are two ways of using the Platform. The first type is consuming content, and the second one is publishing content and engaging with other users.

How Users Consume Content

You need to understand that people consume content differently on different platforms. Combining Instagram and YouTube, for example, would make no sense. Users who visit YouTube intend to watch videos for an extended period. Nobody visits Instagram to watch a 25-minute long 'try not to laugh' video.

Instagram is a visually heavy platform. Users want to look at pretty pictures, funny videos and exciting things, meaning that people use Instagram to consume images and videos first text second. Looking at a picture takes less than a second, finding out if a short video is worth watching less than 3 seconds. Therefore, people on Instagram consume content fast with a short attention span. Users want to take in as much information as possible in little time. When there is time during breakfast, in the tram, during breaks or in the evening, people glance at their Instagram. The intention might be learning something new, entertainment, finding out what friends are up to, having celebrity-like experiences or to relax.

Pro Tip: Users prefer original content, storytelling, and beliefs. Instagram can be a great place to learn, to get inspired, or to be entertained.

Why Users Publish and Engage

Most users on Instagram are regular users meaning they do not post and engage on the Platform because they want to do business. Every time a user publishes a new post and gets a new like, a new comment or a new follower, his dopamine spikes. Dopamine is like an excitement drug. Every time a user receives a dopamine rush, he feels great.

Dopamine also spikes if users share their opinion, participate in a controversial discussion, guess or contribute. It's exciting to be part of a community. It feels great to be right. If a user is currently living with problems, it feels good to have somebody to relate to, to share a situation, or to look up to someone who already pushed through it. Due to that, our brains know that checking Instagram gives us a fast and simple dopamine boost.

Chapter 5: Creating Your Account, Profile Picture, And Bio

So, you're sold on the power of Instagram but don't know how to get started. Welcome to the nuts and bolts of the Instagram platform.

Step 1: Create your account

The first and most important thing to start with is creating a separate account for Instagram. While you can't make a specific business account with Instagram, your business account needs to be separate from your personal account if you have one. Taking pictures of your cat may be fun, but unless you're selling cat toys you probably want to refrain from posting this on your business Instagram feed. (Of course, if you are in a pet-related business this is a good idea. If you're selling car parts, it's probably less of a draw.)

Of course, you still want your brand to appear human, but posting pictures of your dinner when your business sells purses isn't the right tack to take.

Keep your business account separate from your personal account. While there's nothing wrong with posting pictures of Fluffy to Instagram, keep that in a personal account rather than your business one unless Fluffy is relevant to your business.

Fortunately, creating an account with Instagram couldn't be easier. All you need to do is download the Instagram App to your smartphone (it works on both Android and iOS) and follow the instructions to set up your account.

However, wait! What's your profile name going to be? Remember that the Instagram presence of, say, Microsoft is under "Microsoft" and not "Bill Gates." While Bill Gates is certainly a recognizable name… it's the business that's being promoted, not Bill Gates.

Thus, you should choose a name that reflects your business. Obviously, it would be ideal if you could get an Instagram handle that would be the exact same name as your business, but this is not always possible. Sometimes, somebody else may have already taken the name that you wish to choose. For instance, somebody named Bob who sells widgets in a different state may have already taken "bobswidgets".

If this happens to you, try choosing a name that includes your business name and another identifying moniker. An example of this may be "Bobswidgetsboston," which would be a good choice for a person named Bob who sells widgets in Boston.

Choose a name that is easily recognizable and directly connected to your brand. You want potential customers to be aware that you are a business and not a personal Instagram account.

That's it! You're in!

Step 2: Add an Appropriate Profile Photo to Your Account

This is an absolute must. Remember that Instagram is a visual medium, so you need to have your profile photo be something good!

Depending on your business, what's appropriate here may be different. If you are an individual consultant, for instance, a picture of yourself may be the best choice. In this case, you are your brand, so your face should show up in your profile picture.

However, if you look at the Instagram accounts of major companies, most of them don't have anybody's face as the profile picture. Think about it - McDonald's is internationally known, but do you know what the CEO looks like? Very likely not. Thus, it would make no sense for McDonald's to have the CEO as the profile picture. The Golden Arches is more appropriate since that is the "face" of the brand.

Either way, make sure that this photo is professional. This is the thumbnail that will appear beside every single post or interaction that you have on Instagram. It literally is your "face" on Instagram, so make it count!

So you need to spend some time figuring out what the "face" of your brand is. If the face of your brand is, indeed, you, then your face should be in the profile picture. If the face of your brand is a logo, then the profile picture should be that logo. Whatever is the most visually recognizable part of your business should be what goes in the profile picture.

Step 3: Create a great bio and add a link!

Next, you have a small amount of space to write a bio. This bio will appear next to your profile picture - you want the text here to be short and snappy. Remember that Instagram is a photo-based medium, not a text-based one. You do not want to write a novel here. Just one or two sentences about your company will do.

Additionally, hashtags have no power in bios. We will talk more about hashtags later on in this guide, but in terms of your bio they have no purpose, so leave them out.

You will want to keep the tone of your bio light and interesting. Do not go too salesy with the language in your bio. If you are truly unsure where to start, you can't fail by using the formula "what you do plus who you are plus something interesting."

So, if you're Bob selling widgets from Boston, you might try, "Hi, I'm Bob, and I've got the best widgets in Boston. Go Celts!" This is informative, to the point, and also has a pop of personality - from this, you can tell that Bob is probably a sports fan.

Do not forget to add a link to your bio. You get one link in your bio. You can certainly change this link to go to different places as is necessary. Probably the most common link would be to the homepage of your independent business website, but there are several different approaches that you can take to this.

For instance, if you are running a promotion and you want your customers to go to the landing page of that promotion, then the link should be to the page of the promotion. This also goes for contests or any other hot-button topics. Remember that this link can be changed at any time - you absolutely can use this to your advantage. This will be discussed later on in the eBook.

However, if you're just starting out on Instagram, the most logical link would be to your homepage. This way, when customers visit your profile you can send them directly to your company. Instant conversion!

In the case of Bob's Widgets from Boston, a sensible link would be "www.bobswidgets.com" for the majority of the time. In the event that Bob were running a promotional event, he might change the link to "www.bobswidgets.com/promotion" or whatever he's trying to direct potential customers to.

Now that you've got your profile set up along with a great profile picture and a snappy, informative bio with accompanying link, you're ready to get started with Instagram!

Chapter 6: Influencer Marketing

Influencer marketing is a great way to get your company name and brand moving around the internet. While it may seem ridiculous to pay someone to promote your product through their social media, if you have someone with millions of followers wearing your products or talking about how much they enjoy working with your business, it's going to reach a broad spectrum of people.

You may be wondering how you could even go about getting an ambassador for your brand. Do you have to reach out to individuals? Do you know who the right person for your company would be? Where is the best place to start on the topic? The good news is that you really don't have to do any of that work. While you can go that route, it tends to be more challenging to get people to respond, and they might not necessarily be the right candidate to help you get your business going. There are several websites that can act as a middleman between you and the influencer. Those companies would have access to much more information about the individual, and you wouldn't have to worry about the ambassador's level of competence when it comes to the promotion of your brand. If they are working with a promotion company, then they know how to use their online presence to your company's advantage.

Instagram is one of the best platforms for utilizing influencer marketing. Instagram has around 800 million users every month. Facebook has a larger user base than Instagram, but Instagram users tend to be more engaged online. It is more effective for marketers to use Instagram because it has the highest interaction rate compared to all other social media platforms. Interaction between companies and customers makes it easier for shoppers to convert to customers. More users are interactive on the Instagram platform, which is why they don't tend to mind when influencers are promoting products. It has been documented that 65% of the top-performing posts include advertised products. It's a win-win for the parties on either side of the advertising.

Using influencers to market your products can be very profitable if done correctly. You have to make sure that you are using the right person who is in a similar niche as the items you are trying to promote. If the influencer already has a following that trusts what they are saying about the product, then you already have a foot in the door when it comes to closing the sale. You might want to continue to work with the same influencer over time to market different products. Once you have developed a good business relationship with them, it can benefit both the influencer and your business to continue promotions together. As people watch someone online and try and recreate looks or find products that they recommend, they tend to stick with the same person. They usually like the product, and it creates a connection between the influencer and the viewer; perhaps they like the same things, or the viewer likes the influencer's personality. Thus, they will continue to watch their videos and share the content which features your product.

Using Ambassadors to Build Your Brand

Like any marketing campaign, when you begin using a new resource, it's important to set goals for what you're looking to accomplish. Your goals need to be measurable. For instance, if you start running promotions through an ambassador program, then you should create a discount code using their name as a special ID; this way, you know whether people are coming to the website due to the ambassador's advertising or not. It also makes it easier for you to determine the benefit of using a particular Instagram influencer. If the product promotion doesn't seem to be working after a period of time, you might want to rethink your strategy. Come up with a new advertisement plan using that influencer, or switch influencers to try and reach a more receptive group of people.

When you begin looking for influencers, if you decide not to use a company middleman, then you need to look at the different aspects of what that influencer does. You need to know what the influencer's niche is. What is it that they specialize in talking about, and what are most of their posts and videos about? If you are a food marketer, then you might want to try and find a food blogger to talk about your work. You'll also want to study their reach. How many followers do they have? How many average likes and reposts do their posts have? If there aren't many people looking at their page or commenting on their work, then it isn't going to be doing your company a lot of good to use them for advertisement.

Another thing to notice is their voice. The way a person speaks or writes says a lot about them. Do they write passionately about the products they have, or are they just reading off of a script and giving you the basics? You want someone who is energetic to promote you; their enthusiasm will spread to other people and encourage them to seek out your product because the influencer was so excited to share that information with them. Their voice can still be professional and sell a big-ticket product if they know how to advertise correctly.

Next, you'll want to look into their engagement rate. Instagrammers like engagement. It's a more active form of social media, and with so many different capabilities from live videos to stories, it's important that the influencer is engaging with their followers. There are online calculators you can use in order to get the minimum amount of interaction an influencer should be using on their page in order to achieve the results that you are looking for.

Once you choose your influencer, it's time to set up a plan on how you want to achieve your goals. Again, there are some legal aspects that go into this section of the work that you have to be cautious of because it does come down to usage rights and payment for services. All of those should be discussed with a company HR representative or lawyer prior to signing an agreement.

The Influencer Marketing Hub says that these five things are the most crucial to getting your influencer to work for you ("The Beginner's Guide to Influencer Marketing", 2018):

Set a Time Frame — Create a reasonable time frame. You don't want the production to take too long, but you also don't want a rushed video when you are paying for promotion. It might be helpful for them to have check-in points, like when they complete the rough draft, so you can give them the time to make any edits before posting.

Content Production — How do you want the influencer to promote the product? Do you want them to use the product in a video? Do you want to have them display it and talk about it and the benefits? Make sure you give the influencer clear instructions on how you want them to make the photo or video to best promote the product.

Content Usage — When it comes to content usage you need to think in advance about what else you may want to use this advertisement for. If you want to use it on other platforms, then you'll want full usage rights. This is something you'll want to discuss with your business and include in the contract for the influencer to sign as well.

Compensation — There are different ways you can pay an influencer, and it should be discussed and finalized before you begin working together. You could either pay them based on their performance and the results of the campaign, or you could pay them a flat fee per post that they do for your company. Whichever way you decide to do it, make sure to lay it all out in a finalized contract before starting.

FTC Regulations — As far as FTC (Federal Trade Commission) regulations go, your influencer has to disclose that they are being sponsored by your company when they give the product review. For the security of the influencer and the company, it's important to know the full outline of the regulations to make sure that you are following any and all rules that are incorporated.

Influencer marketing is a great way to get the message about your product or company out. If you're just starting up on a new campaign, or even trying to get more followers and likes on your personal Instagram account, having someone help build your company's reputation is definitely going to help. While new followers may not know much about your company at first, influencers are definitely capable of swaying the public into a simple click to follow a page. They can be a great way for people to learn about your company and products, even in passing. They might be scrolling past your posts on their news feed at first, but then they will see the posts pop up. It all ties together with what you post as well. If your company is posting interesting or exciting photos and videos with dominant and eye-capturing shots, then your followers will stop to read and view those posts.

Chapter 7: Marketing With Instagram

Instagram is heavily used by people who are just starting up a business for promoting their product. The reason for this is that it is so easy for your posts to be seen by people around the world due to fewer restrictions on privacy policies, and the people not having to be on your follower's list to see your items. However, to succeed, you really have to be seen by a lot of people. To do this, you need to up your following. These tips will help you up your following and market your product or brand on Instagram with ease.

Utilize the Trends

The latest thing these days are hashtags. They can link you to other people posting about the same things as you. These little tags are also easily searchable, and people often just do a search on them to see what people are posting about their favorite things. This makes it essential for you to use hashtags that are popular and trending. Even just using the generally popular ones is better than using nothing at all in the way of getting noticed.

There are a few that you should use on a regular basis, as they are popular no matter what is going on in the world. Using these hashtags will get you noticed by a lot more people than posting without hashtags.

☐ **#Love:** This hashtag may seem a little silly, but it is used by over a million people a day and brings in a lot of attention to people who use it. People who share posts with this hashtag are usually so tired of seeing negative posts that they want to spread some positivity in the world by showing off things that they love. By using this hashtag, you are making your post public for millions of people to see, which is what you want, because that will bring you in more followers, and more followers mean more business.

The best way to share this hashtag is with a cute photo of a pet. People go gaga over pets and cute animal photos. Baby animals are the best. Share a photo of your pet (if you have one) representing your brand with a caption talking about how your pet #loves to support you. People eat things like that up, and can't get enough of it.

☐ **#Me:** This one is one of the more popular ones because people love to show off sides of themselves that maybe not everyone knows about already. They like to be real. Millions of users use this hashtag each week. It just goes to show how easy it is to be open and raw about yourself behind a screen. However, not everyone uses this hashtag for heartfelt confessions. Some share a meme with the caption "this so #me" And that is okay too. However, if you are looking to represent your brand using these hashtags, maybe you should share a picture of yourself doing something wacky that you enjoy doing and caption it about how it is you doing something that you enjoy taking a break from work for a little fun. You don't have to rep your brand constantly in your pictures. Mention the brand when you say you are taking a break from work.

☐ **#TBT:** This is one of the most popular hashtags out there. In fact, it has spread to other social media sites as well, such as Facebook and Twitter. Everyone loves to do the #TBT posts. (Throwback Thursday). These posts usually involve someone posting a picture of themselves as a kid or with an old group of friends with the caption "Those were the days #TBT

If you want to use this caption, you could try posting an old photo of yourself with a caption like "#TBT to back before I was a successful entrepreneur with my own company."

☐ **#Cute:** This one is kind of self-explanatory, but there is a little more to it than you think. This hashtag is used by several million people a day because let's face it. No matter how goth we were in high school, everyone loved pictures of cute little babies and puppies playing with kittens. Those adorable photos that make you go awe. When using this hashtag, try using it without representing your brand. Just share a photo that you think is cute and caption it using that hashtag. It will give your page a nice breather from all of the marketing posts, and liven it up a little bit.

I know you are wondering why you would post something that doesn't have to do with your brand but trust me on this, it will bring you in more followers. When you can expect everything to be the same, then you really just don't become interested anymore. Not only will you get new followers, but your current ones won't get fed up with the same old posts and just up and unfollow you due to being done with your posts. Your new followers will still see that you are a business and will still check you out, as they decided to follow you anyway, so it is a win win situation.

☐　**#L4l:** This stands for "Like for a Like" which means that you go through and like someone's pictures, and for every one that you like, they have to like one of yours. This is one of the most searched hashtags because people love to get noticed and get likes on their pictures. It is also helpful because when someone likes something, all their followers can see that they liked it, so a like for like gives you both publicity without the commitment of a follow or a share. Like for likes are used by a lot of people to boost not only their followers but the people participating's followers due to the discovery option that shows their followers what was liked. It is a win for all parties involved.

☐ **#S4s:** This is, you guessed it "Share for a Share." This popular hashtag involves both parties sharing the other person's profile via what is called a "shout out." These shout outs bring both parties viewers because all of their collective followers can see these. Which means that the both parties get more views because the followers of the person who shared the shout out can see that they should check out the new person, and the followers of the new person can see that someone else is worth following. If you both do shout outs, as is the case in a share for share, you have twice the chance of getting more followers. This is always desirable, as people love being mentioned in other people's posts, and they love gaining new followers.

If you do enough S4S posts, then eventually you could catch the eye of a sponsor. Sponsors can do things like back you monetarily, or even do a simple thing like share you on their page that probably has millions of followers, so that you can gain more followers.

☐ **#FF:** This stands for Follow Friday, and is a very popular hashtag on none other than Friday itself. This hashtag involves the poster promising to follow people back if they meet the requirements to earn a follow. These requirements are generally just to follow the person back, but sometimes they might be to like a certain amount of pictures, comment your name, and then follow. It all just depends on who is posting it.

Follow Fridays are popular because everyone loves to gain new followers, and most of the time they don't mind liking a few pictures to gain followers. It all depends on the person though. Some people don't want to jump through hoops, they just want to get new followers without doing anything.

☐   **#F4F:** That is where the follow for a follow comes in. This popular hashtag is for people who want new followers for doing nothing but following another person's profile. This hashtag is frequented by millions of users on a regular basis, and it allows people to get more followers than most hashtags, because all they have to do is hit that follow button, and then they too gain a follower.

Be careful when posting this, however, because some people only follow you for long enough for you to follow them, then they unfollow you. Always keep track of who followed you after an F4F post, and make sure that they don't unfollow you in a few days' time. If they do unfollow you, simply unfollow them.

These are some hashtags that you can use, and they are generally pretty popular.

When in doubt, trend it out. This means that if you do not know what hashtag to use, look at what is trending at that time. Trending hashtags generally have to do with what is going on in the world at the time. Hashtags are very useful, but only if used well. There are some tips that you should know that will help you master this new trend of hyper linking your post to others with a word.

When posting with hashtags, always know that more is better. You can combine two or three similar hashtags to get people's attention. Hashtags such as #love and #cute go together pretty well. You want people to view you, and the more hashtags you use, the more dark spots in search you cover. You will pop up in multiple different searches, which will make more people interested in you.

However, there is such a thing as too much of a good thing. When using hashtags, be careful not to string too many together to the point where it is hard to tell what you are trying to say. This is a common problem with a lot of people who are using hashtags. They want to come up with a bunch of searches so they just start using hashtags, even if the hashtags are something no one would ever think to search. Here is an example post if someone is posting a picture of themselves out side:

"Oh my goodness! It is such a #beautiful day out today! #Nice #Outdoors #Me #sundress #boots #cute #love #lovethisweather #lovethisoutfit #imsocute #longhashtagsarefun #youcantbeatmyhashtag #gorgeousday

By the time this post is over, you can't discern if it is about the nice day. The person's outfit, long hashtags or what it is. Stay away from using more than two or three hashtags at a time. There is a fine line between smart use and over use. You have to walk that line like you are on a tight rope with no net below you. This is important because if you go over, no one will pay attention to your post, and if you go under, not a lot of people will pay attention to your post. If the hashtags are too relevant to what you alone are posting then you will not get any attention, if they are not relevant enough, then you will not get any attention. It is a tight line you have to walk, but if you follow these tips, you should be okay.

Be human in your posts. Don't use hashtags like a robot. Give the people what they want, but keep a little of yourself in there too, because people love the human element. Share some jokes, maybe a cute picture or two that doesn't relate to your brand, and allow your posts to connect with your audience. You want them to feel connected too. That is how you gain the most followers. Make people feel like they are connected and important.

When using hashtags, try to use ones that are easily searchable, and have a good amount of traffic. If you are constantly making up your own, no one is going to know to search for that hashtag. You have to use what is trending to your advantage. It is okay to create maybe one or two hashtags for your brand to make it easily searchable, but other than that stick with the flow of what is already going on.

Now that you know how to avoid being a #disaster when using hashtags, you will be able to make posts with confidence knowing that you know the keys to making your posts visible. You don't have to hashtag every post, just occasionally try to add a few hashtags.

Chapter 8: Hacks For Video Views On Instagram

These hacks I'm about to share are guaranteed to work because with each video I've posted on my own page, I've received over twenty-five thousand views for every single video. Wowsa.

Number one: is choosing a great Instagram video cover. This should entice viewers to want to click and watch the video, especially if your video is a little way down the feed.

Number two: is every time you make a post, be it a video or even an image; you should take a screenshot and upload it to your Instagram story. On top of this, you need to place an arrow which points toward your name. This is a gentle reminder for people to click on your profile. When you do this, it is placed in feeds and also in the story, so it doubles your chances of them visiting your page and **liking** your video too. What this does is sneakily add a lot more interaction to your page.

Number three: isn't so much a hack as it is a secret. If you can gain enough video views fast enough, you can make your way to the **Instagram Explorer Page**, and once your video is on there, there are many more thousands of people viewing your video. As an example, a regular video which receives around twenty-thousand views can explode and receive almost one-hundred thousand views from being on this page.

Number four: you need to create an Instagram group, and here you gather around twenty to thirty people, and each time one of the group posts something, all the others go to the page and **like**, view, and comment on the video or image. This is a great way to help each other grow together.

Number five: is an easy way to continually drive traffic. Each time you post, ta"I see no ships, only hardships."g five people. And if you have a group, you should tag five of these; as well as five other people (even if they are at random). This makes them wonder who has tagged them and they visit your page and then end up watching your video... hopefully!

Number six: isn't always easy for a lot of people as it involves the use of an email list. If you happen to have one, you can inform all of these people you have a new post by dropping them a quick email to let them know.

Number seven: requires you to do a shoutout with one person every day. This helps to increase daily traffic; thus increasing video views. This is even more helpful when you've just made a post. Actually, this can create lots of traffic, and if there are plenty of people watching your video, you might even find yourself on the **Instagram Explorer Page**.

Getting 20K "Organic" Instagram Followers One of the most important tips for increasing followers are shoutouts, and if you have (for example) a thousand followers who might have taken you two to three months to build, you could increase this big time. When you shoutout to other followers who have similar numbers of viewers, this can give exponential growth to the numbers of your followers. As an example of how this works, when two music artists collaborate they bring with them both sides of their fan base. From this point, there are double the people who are exposed to the other artist's music. This is what happens on Instagram, and it shows why shoutouts are vitally important.

The second thing is: to make sure you follow and promote people who relate to you, your product/s, or your service/s. As these people already have a following of people who are in tune with what they are doing, these followers are more likely to be interested in what you have to say, as well. It is common sense to stick with your topic, and it's a "shot in the dark" if you receive feedback from another person (or their followers) and they are totally unrelated.

My next tip is all about the importance of comments. An image can have one thousand **likes**, with a mere one hundred comments. So when you have commented on a person's image, rather than just clicking **like**, they will appreciate the effort you have taken to leave this comment. Now, hopefully they will respond in the same way to your images. If you are not sure this would work, think of how you feel when a person leaves a comment on your images, compared to just leaving a **like** on your image. Doesn't it make you feel all tingly? So, this is a good tip that works really well, in my opinion.

Next is all about the effort, when you take pictures to post, these should not only be high resolution, but they should show they have been made with some forethought, as well. There are phones which take great pictures, but this isn't enough. If you add filters and make them look arty, they grab more attention than a simple selfie. People like to see good pictures, and if you post a simple selfie it seems lazy, and this reflects on your profile and doesn't give a person a reason to follow you. You want to stand out from the crowd as much as possible.

Easy profile names are my next tip. These should be as concise as possible, easy to remember, and easy to search. The reason being is; if it's too long (or the spelling isn't that easy), people won't know how to spell it to search for you. If this is the case, they'll give up before trying to find out where you're at. So, this is really worth remembering.

Next, you should create a system and a habit which you perform every day. A prime example is to DM (direct message) a set number of people every day. Once you've done this, they will visit your page to see who has messaged them directly. If you say something nice to them, it can bring new people and followers (all the time) to your page. Secondary to this is the **likes** of over ten (and up to a hundred) pictures per day. Out of these, you should comment on around twenty of these pictures. For a small amount of effort, you could gain a considerable amount of followers.

Your profile picture needs to be something which makes people want to click on it and then go on to visit your page. This is even more important when you show up in a person's feed, mostly because your thumbnail needs to catch their attention.

Hopefully, they'll want to know more of what is behind the image. If you only have a regular picture of yourself, there's more of a chance your post will be skimmed over (as well as them not visiting your page afterward).

My next point is all about numbers, and where big isn't always better, as you might've heard many times over. It might seem the more people you follow, the better your chances. This isn't the case, actually, because if you follow everyone, people look at you as following for "following's sake." I personally found a sweet spot of not following more than two thousand people. Once you go over this number of two thousand, you start to look like a spammer, and people tend not to follow you for this very reason.

Here is another sneaky trick. When you reach around five thousand or ten thousand followers, switch to **private**. Now, inside your bio, you need to say a person should follow you to see your "secret" profile. This raises a person's curiosity, and they'll generally follow you to see what is hidden from view. It might be the case they unfollow you after ten minutes once they look at your profile, but that doesn't matter, and the main thing is they followed you in the first place. On top of this, you shouldn't accept them for around two hours, this will delay them thinking about unfollowing you. It is kinda sneaky, but it does work well.

Getting a Shoutout from Big Pages

If you can do this, you can see up to three thousand people following you in a single day because you've gained a shoutout from a bigger page. If you do get one of these shoutouts, your growth happens exponentially, and this happens because the followers of the big pages are looking for people to follow. You can see that it works, especially if you are female. This you can see from models' pages because they have tons of followers, generally speaking.

To do this, make a list of all the pages which have the potential of shouting you out. These should be pages which relate to you (or your business). The tip now is to tag each post of yours with all of the pages on your list. This can be done quickly and is super-easy to perform.

On top of this, you'll need to keep track of the pages you've tagged. Rather than making a list, it is much easier to bookmark them in your browser. This is a reminder of the pages you need to tag, and you can quickly open them to check their new images and begin chatting to them all from one click.

The real secret here is building relationships to gain these shoutouts. Now you can DM these pages and drop hints you want a shoutout from them too. It won't take them long to respond. There is also the option of asking how much they'd charge you for a shoutout (if they won't do it for free). It might cost up to twenty dollars; not bad if you can gain a couple of hundred extra followers from doing so.

Chapter 9: Use It All Even If You Are On The Right Track, You'll Get Run Over If You Just Sit There." – Will Rodgers

"Algorithm" is a word that can strike fear to even the most avid social media users. When it comes to Instagram, we have to play by the rules of the people running this app. We have to do whatever we can to help make our posts shine and rank better in the algorithm. In the previous chapter we have already touched on some important points on how to do this, such as longer captions and posting consistently. But another important element to improve your ranking and to also increase your chances of making sales is to use every facet of Instagram and all the content opportunities it provides. This includes: stories, live and IGTV.

Instagram stories

When stories were first introduced to the platform in 2016, it confused a lot of people. Many users passed it off as a cheap copy of Snapchat. Fast forward to 2020 and Snapchat is almost non-existent while Instagram stories continues to thrive. In fact, some users are now looking at stories more than they are scrolling through their feed!

When it comes to running ads on Instagram (more on that in chapter 8), it's also the place I've been getting the most link clicks for myself and my clients. People who watch are more engaged, they click on links and they purchase the products they see there. If you aren't using Instagram stories, you're just leaving money on the table.

One of the most interesting and little known points about stories is that it can also help improve the engagement on your feed posts. We now live in an era where people are liking and commenting less on Instagram posts. However, reactions, replies and clicks on stories are only increasing. You are much more likely to receive a response on a story than a post. People are interactive there when it comes to polls and Q&A's but it also takes a lot of pressure off being able to reply to someone privately instead of commenting publicly. And when people are engaging with your stories, the Instagram algorithm recognises that and it will see that people love your content and it will start pushing your feed posts up higher. The theory is if someone loves your stories and is actively interacting with you there, the algorithm knows your follower likely wants to see what you're posting on your feed.

This only further enforces how important stories are and how if you're not using them, you're also restricting the reach of your feed posts.

Instagram live

When it comes to social media, I absolutely love video. I believe video is the future of online marketing and it's something every business should be investing in. But I will admit that live video is a whole different ball game. It certainly makes me nervous! In fact, the second time I tried going live, I lent my phone on what I thought was a great little stand but didn't realise it blocked the microphone and no one could hear what I was saying. It was pretty embarrassing and obviously it's something you can't edit out when it's live. However, I still continue to show up and try to go live every once in a while because I know it's worth the extra effort. It's a great way to build a connection to your followers in a fun and casual setting. Plus, it doesn't have to be perfect because it's only available to replay for 24 hours. Another added bonus is that when you go live, a selection of your followers will be sent a push notification inviting them to come watch your live. This is a rare and incredible opportunity to directly ask your followers to visit your page. Your followers usually only get notifications for your account if they specifically make the effort to visit your page and turn on notifications for your posts and stories. When you go live however, they will get notified and your live stream will also sit at the front of the list of Instagram stories on their home page, meaning it's the first thing they will see when they open the app. Instagram goes to a lot of effort to promote live streams so you should definitely take advantage of that.

But most importantly, you are once again showing the algorithm that your followers love to consume any and all of your content. This will once again lead to more engagement on your feed posts and more views on your stories.

IGTV

Instagram TV still feels relatively new to the platform even though it was introduced in 2018. This was Instagram's way of competing with YouTube by offering a place to watch longer videos. While videos posted to your feed are limited to 1 minute, on IGTV they can be up to 10 minutes long.

Once uploaded, your IGTV can be shared directly to your feed to promote it and it's value continues to increase. It's been common knowledge in the marketing world for years now that video is a very engaging form of content. A recent study of Instagram found video posts have 38% higher rates of engagement than image posts - how amazing is that? Similar to using live video, IGTV allows your customers to see you in a whole new light. An image can be static, it doesnt give away much but a video allows your customers to see you or your product up close and in action. It's important to take advantage of this video option on the Instagram platform to build that loyal connection with your followers.

IGTV content can be more time consuming to create. You will need to brainstorm a solid idea and perhaps even write a script if there is going to be a lot of talking involved. It also usually requires a little more editing if you want to create something that's engaging enough to keep people watching for the full 10 minutes. If adding IGTV into your business marketing plan sounds a bit overwhelming, I'd recommend starting off with just setting a goal to publish one per month.

But wait, there's more…

By the time I publish this ebook, I bet Instagram will have come up with some hot new addition to their app so make sure you're using that too! Better yet, jump on it early. Those who were the first to adapt to Instagram Stories and start using them while everyone else was still committed to Snapchat ended up in a better place. Be a pioneer, not another follower of the herd.

Chapter 10: The Best Tips For Growing Your Instagram Business Account

Now that we have had some time to learn what Instagram is all about and all of the great ways that it is able to help us to add to our marketing plan without having to spend a lot of extra money on a social media expert. But even though we need some of the basics, what are some of the things that you are able to do in order to make yourself stand out on Instagram so that your potential customers would choose you over someone else. Some of the best tips that you can do in order to help grow your Instagram business account include:

Connect Facebook and Instagram together: these two social media sites are actually connected and when you let them work together, you will find that they can be really powerful tools. Make sure that Instagram and Facebook are connected so that you can get the best from both of them and boost some of the marketing efforts. You can even add in a tab for Instagram on your Facebook page so that when you post something on Instagram, it will automatically link up with the Facebook and send it over, saving you time.

Create your strategy: as a business owner, you need to make sure that you have a good brand strategy that is going to help your business to grow. You will want to make sure that whatever strategy you start to use on Instagram is going to keep the focus on the brand that you have built and how that brand sees the world. Instagram is great for sharing videos and photos so make sure that when you connect the business with your followers, make sure that it stays consistent with your brand rather than straying away or showing things that just don't go together.

Use your brand or company name in hashtags: the hashtags that you pick don't have to be complicated. If you already have a pretty good following on Instagram, or your brand name is well known, go ahead and use this as one of your hashtags. This will make it easier for your followers to find you because they can just search the name and find some of your posts.

Make a follower famous: it is not just about your followers checking out your posts, it is about how you interact with your followers. Take the time to look over the pages of your followers and then like and share some of their posts. This helps to show the customers that you really appreciate them because you are acknowledging their cool posts and sharing them with others on your page. Be careful with this one though because some may be personal and you should always ask for permission beforehand if you are unsure whether they would like it shared or not.

Be creative with the pictures: it is not enough to just take a few pictures of your products or services and then call it good. You need to get a bit creative. There are thousands of pictures of food or sweaters and so on, how are you going to make your pictures draw the attention of the customers that you want? You can use filters, different angles, changing the lighting, and some of the other tricks on photography to help you out. you don't need to hire a professional photography to do this, but you should be a bit creative with what you are doing.

Work on videos: a new feature that you are able to find with Instagram is that now you can add videos to your postings. This is a new way to interact with your customers, telling them about some of the products, bringing up rules about a promotion, or doing something else that is creative. Just like with the photos that you post, the videos need to have something to do with the business, but it is fine to be a bit creative with this.

Think about how to show your products: remember that as a business, you need to make sure that you are showcasing some of the products that you sell. Show these products in a bunch of different ways. This is a mobile site so be creative when showing it off, but many times businesses see success when they show the products in real life, such as something wearing the sweater on a walk rather than just having it lay there.

Post some good videos (or you): if you are the CEO of your business, this means you need to post a few videos of yourself. This is meant to make the top executive of the company look personable. Make some short and even some quirky videos of the

CEO to add to Instagram. Showing some of your hobbies outside of work, for example, can be a lot of fun.

Partner with some other brands: this can be beneficial for both you and for the other brands that you decide to work with on this promotion. If the two of you are reaching for similar customers but are different products, it can make it easier to find customers that both of you can use. Partner up with a few other brands and have them post some of your products on their feeds while you do the same for them.

Post on a consistent basis: it is not going to do well for your business if you just post for a few days here and there, ignore the profile for awhile, come back for a week, and then ignore it again, keeping up on this same cycle for the next few years. If you want to find more followers and get more customers, you need to post with some consistency. You can even post some of the same things on Instagram more than once, just make sure that you find a good rhythm to when you post. Sure there will be days when you miss out because you get busy, but make sure to keep up with this as much as possible.

Track your results: how are you supposed to know if what you are doing is successful if you aren't keeping track of what is going on with analytics and other tracking tools. You should use some of the tracking tools that are available through Instagram and monitor when is the best time for you to post, what your followers like the most, and other things that make it easier for you to get better results in the future.

Host a photo contest: there are many options that you can stick with when it comes to having a photo contents. The first option is to have your followers post some pictures of them using your products, and then have a vote on which ones are the best with the winner getting a prize. Sometimes you can post one of your own pictures and have your followers like and share that picture to be entered for a prize as well. Videos can work in much the same way. You can mess around with this one a bit to see what you are able to figure out for terms and prizes, but this is a great way to get people to interact a bit more on your page and to share your products even more.

Keep up with the trends; the trends on social media sites will often change over time. Things that work today may not work as much later in the future. If you refuse to keep up with some of these trends, you are going to start missing out on some of the customers that you need. In some cases, missing out on trends could end up hurting you in trends and search results. The trends can be beneficial to you when it comes to helping your customers and getting ranked higher in the site's search.

Working on Instagram does not have to be something that is difficult or impossible to do, as long as you make a plan and try to showcase your work while interacting with your customer. It will take a bit of time to make this work, but overall, you are going to be able to put your Instagram account to work for you and it will bring in a great conversion rate so your products begin to sell.

Chapter 11: Instagram Hacks For Taking Really Good Photos

If you couldn't get this until now, Instagram is a great place to market your business. The photo sharing platform has all the right tools for promoting your brand. However, since the majority of the posts on this platform are photos, how can you stand out among the tough competition out there?

The answer to this is by using good photos for your posts. Making your photos attractive and of the best quality gives you the edge you need to help boost your page.

It is true that your photos must be top-notch but the question is how can you take great photos that will be of the best quality?

Here are some tips that will help you take the best photos:

1. Plan ahead

Planning ahead before taking the picture is a good way to start the process of taking good photos. You are advised to think about your brand and what you really want to offer your audience. Advanced planning gives you a good idea about what you want to do. That will give you a blueprint to work with.

2. Don't be obsessed with people's thoughts

When you are through with your plan, take the time to find you what you really like. Your thoughts shouldn't be focused primarily on what the Instagram community wants from you, or the type of photo is the most popular amongst the members of the community. If you give heed to these thoughts, you will defeat your goal of getting the best picture before you even took out the camera.

3. Use natural sources of light

One of the most important factors you must consider is lighting. It is the key to the overall beauty of your photos. Note that even the best photo-editing app with the most complex filter can never make a good job of a poorly-lit photo. Using natural sources of light will give your photos the right illumination. If you must take any photo outdoors, you should consider doing so early in the morning, late in the afternoon, or overcast days. These periods are when you can get the best shots.

4. Use your eyes before your camera

Your eyes still remain an important and efficient tool for taking good photos. It is customary to see people taking a couple of pictures, comparing them, and then making their choice. Instead of towing that path and wasting time taking tens of shots before settling for the best, use your eyes before using the camera.

This requires that you look at the object critically, frame the picture with your eyes, and observe the object for some time. This may give you a new perspective for looking at the object so that you can get the best shot after taking a few pictures.

5. Use the grid feature

It is good to bring your composition in when attempting to take a picture. Whenever you want to take a picture, you can make the best job of it by turning on the grid. You can watch the elements overlapping through your viewfinder or on the screen until you get the perfect conditions for shooting. That will enhance the beauty of your photo.

6. Use the point of interest

A common feature of all good photos is the presence of a point of interest. It may be someone in the foreground or a great landscape with sharp lines that focuses the viewer's eyes. Great photos are known for having more than one point of interest without them overlapping and creating a sense of clutter. Try to let your photo reveal a little information about the place or person. Let it tell a story about the point of interest.

7. Watch out for moments

Another way to make your photo great is by letting your pictures have great moments. Let the moments be about the subjects or subject you want to shoot. Look for some natural moments such as extreme, peak, settled, or emotional moments. Either of these moments will make the picture interesting.

If there are unwanted pieces of information, stay away from them. The unwanted information may detract from the great moment and impact the picture negatively. You can only be pardoned if the unwanted information contributes to the overall beauty of the image.

Your goal is to have a clean image, free of unwanted clutter, that draws the attention of the viewers directly to the story you want to tell.

8. Strong shapes, colors, and lines are good

One of the qualities of a good Instagram image is strong colors and well-defined lines. The photo should contain some elements that will loom large in your camera's frame so that it can easily draw the attention of the viewers. Through personal training and regular practice, you will develop the skills for conveying some emotions with your pictures.

9. Use third-party apps

There are tons of third-party apps that you can use to make your pictures stand out. These apps come in different forms and for a wide variety of functions. You can explore the functionalities of these apps to add to the overall beauty of your images.

An app that is good for simulating a slow shutter to some moving objects, such as blurry water, can create a long-exposure effect. The effect will be more pronounced on waterfalls or incredibly large bodies of water. That will give you the perfect condition to show high contrast between the sharp, still surroundings and the water.

10. Use light from strange sources

If you compare your phone camera with traditional cameras, you will see a clear distinction. The lens of the phone camera has a different way of absorbing light than the camera. That makes it possible for the phone camera to see light from some strange places such as behind the object or above it.

If you move the object around without taking your eyes off it through your phone camera, you will see the object as it transforms until you can see the rays of light on your lens. The light will have a powerful impact on the image. This is the moment you are waiting for. Take your shot right here.

11. Leverage the burst mode

When taking a picture, you may see the need to make a moment stand still without losing its detail. If you want to do that, shoot in daylight or in a well-lit space so that you can use a fast shutter speed.

Ensure that you tap the screen to make it possible to lock focus on the object manually. You can also make the exposure perfect by using the slide bar before taking the shot. With burst mode, you have a perfect tool that will be useful when choosing the most appropriate moment for the picture.

12. Shoot from a wide variety of angles

You can try to take your pictures from viewpoints that look quite unusual. If you consider a view to be normal, it can actually look awesome if you shoot it from a different perspective than through the perspective you see.

Consider shooting from as many angles as possible to make your pictures more appealing. You can try the right-down or up-high position and see the impact it has on your image.

13. Use props

You should consider using different objects, and observe their impact on the story you are trying to tell. By taking your environment and the background of the object into consideration, you can do a good job of making your photo look great by making the scene come alive.

14. Use a bad weather to your advantage

While some people curl up at the idea of having to deal with bad weather while shooting, you can use the bad weather to your advantage. Whenever there is fog, snow, or rain you should go out there and find a way to make the best use of that weather to shoot a unique picture. An experienced photographer once suggested that you should use bad weather to make good photographs.

15. Use the puddles after the rain

After a rainfall, go out there and take awesome photos. The puddles will give you reflections that you can utilize to contribute beauty to your pictures. That background will be great for taking interesting pictures and you shouldn't hesitate to use them.

16. Consider using white space

White space is fun to use. They add uniqueness and beauty to your picture. Take a look at some masterpieces like the latest catalog of J.Crew, or an outstandingly beautiful home. What common feature do they have? Both of these use tons of white space.

You can imitate them and bring such an impression to your picture so that you can make your Instagram feed neat and clutter free. How you feel about those pictures when you see them mirrors the way others will feel when viewing your Instagram feed when it has enough white space.

The best way to have a good shot with white space is to look for white backgrounds when shooting. If you want to photograph a person, you can shoot in front of a white wall to have that effect on your picture.

If you want to shoot an object, a white window sill or a piece of foam board should be used for photographing the object in order to add the white space effect.

Some font apps also have such feature. You can try WordSwag and use it to put an impressive quote on your photo to give it that white space effect. That will give your feed some breathing room.

17. Take advantage of the portrait mode

Instagram has a new portrait mode that you can take advantage of. You can use it to lay emphasis on the length of a particular scene. You can also use it to tell a detailed story that just isn't possible with a square crop.

18. Add more elements

Adding more elements to your scale will make your photo look great. Adding scale to your image can be done by simply including a person in the image's frame. You can try different poses within the same scene to find the best one that will add to the beauty of your image.

19. Layers are handy

Using layers for your images makes it possible to convey a perfect message to the viewer. The goal is to let the viewers share the same point of view with you. Using these will give your audience a good view of your brand because they see your brand exactly the way you want them to see it.

20. Use patches of light

You can find patches of light in different places. The street lamp and the rays of sunlight are perfect sources for these patches of light. During a photography session, find them and use them to enhance your skills.

An important attribute of using patches of light emanating from the sun is that the patches will always give you a variety of backgrounds to use. Make use of that to give your audience a perfect picture.

21. Use the dusk to your advantage

Even when the sun is going down you can still stay out to take beautiful pictures. Although we have limited vision when the sun goes down, modern cameras have better ability to pick up light than humans.

This is a good way to give your audience something beautiful. By leveraging the unusual power of the camera to capture the captivating moments of a sunset, you can give your audience something truly amazing.

22. Move as physically possible to your subject

You can get more than you bargain for if you can move closer to your object as much as possible. Whether you want to shoot animals or people, it is advisable that you get close to them. That creates the right emotion and intimacy in your work. Your audience will appreciate the output and the sense of intimacy associated with the picture. Move closer to the object and use the widest focal length you can. That will bring the object into perspective, and will fill the frame of the photo. The result is a subject that is popped out so much that this cannot be achieved without the lens.

If you are an iPhone user, Moment has a good wide angle lens that will give you the best results. On the other hand, DSLR users may find the 16-35 mm lens very useful.

23. Use your phone's accessories

When considering taking a good shot, a lens attachment can make all the difference in improving your photo. If you want to add some character to the photo, consider using a wide angle lens.

24. Your edits should be simple

The availability of different editing tools has turned some people into editing freaks. While some people keep their edits simple, some have a tendency over edit their shots. Experience has shown that over-edited photos can lose its appeal. Therefore, when using filters to give your photos the best look, resist the urge to overdo it.

Whichever editing tool you use, be moderate. Don't push a photo too far from its real natural state. Users won't find it attractive that way. However, subtle tweaks are cool and will help the image to maintain its natural look.

A study by the social media scientist at HubSpot, Dan Zarella, revealed that photos that don't have too much color saturation in them get more likes than the others that are over-edited. What else did the stats say? Such images can get almost 600% likes more than other posts.

25. Always aim for quality

You can up your game on Instagram by curating your feed and making sharing a better part of your activities as opposed to posting. The implication here is that you should be selective about lighting and composition. That will give you tons of high-quality images to choose from to share with your audience.

26. Make practice a way of life

You can't get it right at your first attempt. You need tons of hours of regular practice sessions to master the art of taking beautiful pictures. If you have the time to make regular practices, you will gradually know your tools and the best ways to take amazing shots.

Always be ready to get a good shot whenever an interesting scene, location, moment, or light pops up. Cultivate the habit of doing a good job composing good photos. You can also take a couple of frames of the same object to get the best results while you also pay close attention to the editing.

The results will be sharp, clean photos that will wow you with natural colors and appealing tones.

The hours of practice sessions will be fully rewarding as the appreciation for your posts increase, and as more followers join your base.

Chapter 12: Tracking

In this chapter, we will talk about ways to save money when operating your business. Keep in mind that although this chapter is not Instagram-specific, it will still teach you how to save money when running a company. We have given you every tool required to get you in the best position to start your Instagram business, and now, we will provide you with one of the best tools out there to budget your spending and overall income. As you know, it is one thing to have a budget, and it is another thing to have a proper plan. Sure, you can sit down and say, "I am going to spend an x amount of money on this x amount of money on that" and so on, but without a proper plan and smart budgeting, you are not going to get to the goals what you are looking for, which is why I present to you, the 50/30/20 rule.

But before you get started, make sure that you were able to review your spending, and you have created an idea of what your budget is going to look like. This rule will not work if you do not know where you are starting, so make sure you get that sorted. Also, make sure you have a pretty strong emergency fund before you begin this 50/30/20 rule.

The 50/30/20 Budget Rule

This budgeting rule is one of the best out there, and if you do not believe me, then you should know that Harvard graduate and bankruptcy expert Elizabeth Warren created this rule. This plan is also used by many influential people out there, so there is no denying that this plan works. We always recommend that you follow the 50/30/20 rule for budgeting goals, but if you find something which works better for you, then, by all means, you can use that as well. With that being said, let us get into the meat and potatoes of the rule

50/30/20. Before you start budgeting anything, the first step would be to calculate your after-tax income. Your after-tax income is your paycheck after you get it in your account. Essentially, what after-tax income means is the amount of money you end up getting in your bank account.

This is for people who are employed; figuring out your after-tax income would be effortless since it will be shown to you in your pay stub. On the other hand, if you are self-employed or you have your own business, then your after-tax income would be your net income. This would include your income after paying taxes, paying off your employees, and your profit margin. Mostly, whatever profession you are in, your after-tax income means all the money in your pocket. Once you have managed to figure out your after-tax income, the second step would be to limit all your needs down to 50 % of your after-tax income. Your needs could be your housing, car payments, car insurance, gas, and anything that helps you live your current lifestyle. Your lifestyle needs to fit within the 50 % margin of what is your net income, so if you make $3,000 a month, you should not be spending more than $1,500 a month in keeping your lifestyle afloat.

Now, to further understand this, you must differentiate between needs and wants. Your wants include anything that you can pay later or purchase later on. There is no need to have it every month or to pay for it every month necessarily. An example would be your cable bill. You can live without a cable, and if you can't, then it is not among your needs. Another example of a want would be a monthly subscription to Spotify. Do you need Spotify? Or is it just a want? That is for you to figure out.

On the other hand, a need could be your rent, and you can't live without a home, which is why it makes it a need. Another example would be your credit card, and you can't live without your credit card since you needed to build up a credit, which makes it a need. Everybody's wants and needs are entirely different, so you need to sit down and figure out all your wants and needs.

Also, remember, your needs should not exceed more than 50 % off your after-tax income. If it does, then you are living way above your lifestyle means if you have to cut down on certain things which are causing you to go over budget in your needs. Once you have figured out your needs, and you have put it in 50 % of your after-tax income, we will not talk about your wants. Yes, while budgeting and still enjoying your life and having all the desires that you are looking for, however, it should only be 30 % of your after-tax income. Now on the surface level, this sounds great. You can buy anything you want with 30 % of your income. For you, this could be a new car or new shoes. But wait for a second, there is something you need to find out before you start spending all your money on extravagant things.

Your wants do not include all those wild things which you might be thinking of, and these include your other urgent necessity, such as Netflix subscription or your phone bill. This 30 % of your income will go toward things that make your life convenient and enjoyable, but it is not necessarily something you cannot live without. For clarification, we will give you some examples. Your wants include your gym membership, car repairs, cable bills, and phone bills.

Most people will spend more on their wants than other things, especially in buying the latest clothes or brand new iPhone. We understand you need clothes and communication tools, but you do not need to make it extravagant unless it fits within your budget. Anything like regular clothing fits in your needs, and anything you want needs to be something. We know it is tricky to understand, but if you are having problems understanding it, then please read through it over and over until you do. The best way to understand it would be to ask yourself: do you want it, or do you need it?

Since you have covered up all 50 % and 30 % of income, we now cover the last 20 %. Your previous 20 % will go to all your savings and debt repayments. As we told you before, if you need something to be paid off, then that goes into your needs section. On the other hand, if you have a credit card payment which is just a minimum payment, then that goes into the 20 %. This will not necessarily be a need but more so to pay off and to build credit. The best way to describe 20 % is to know that 20 % will be used to pay off any debts and or to pay your minimum credit card payments, for instance. You should spend that 20 % of your income to pay off your debts, build the emergency funds, and also to build up your retirement funds. Anything extra or additional debt will go into 20 % of your income when it comes to paying off your debt. Do not be confused with 50 % and 20 %, and 50 %. What you will be paying is an absolute necessity; it is something you can't live without. On the other hand, 20 % will be covering things that you want to pay off eventually or to build a certain amount of wealth, and hence, 20 % of your income will go toward your minimum credit card payments or to pay off a small loan. Anyway, before you set up your 50/30/2o budget, find out what your wants are and what your needs are, and then base it off accordingly. Everybody's 50-30-20 budget rule will be a lot different from the other person's budget, which is why it is so unique and works a lot better than any other budgeting rule out there. Sit down and write out all of your wants and needs. Then once you have a great idea of where your money will be going in regards to the 50/30/20 rule, it would be easier for you to start building a vast financial portfolio.

We will now give you an example of a 50/30/20 rule, and hopefully, in this way, you can understand how this would work in a real-life scenario. In this scenario, you make 42,000 a year after-tax or $3,500 a month. You live in a decent-sized home, and you are living by yourself. You drive a fully paid off car, and you are a firm believer in the minimalist lifestyle approach, which means you do not have the habit of spending money on extravagant things in life. However, you like to spend money on traveling, and you also want to watch documentaries on Netflix.

Since you just adopted the minimalist lifestyle, you still have some debt to pay off, one of them being your student loan, which is $10,000 and your credit card, which is $2,000. With this as your living situation, let us break down how you would be able to budget your income accordingly. Since you make $3,500 a month, you can't spend more than $1,750 on your needs, and if you are, then you need to lower your lifestyle needs. Your house costs you $1,000 a month, which is under your needs, and your grocery is $400 a month, which is under your needs, and your minimum credit card payment is also a type of need, which is around $50 a month. Finally, your average spending per month on clothes is $100 a month, summing up your needs to $1,550 a month, which means you have $200 left to spend.

The second thing we need to cover would be the 30 % allocation, and your wants include your phone bill, which is $50, and your Netflix subscription, which is $7 a month. Your internet is $50 a month, and your utilities, such as gas, electricity, water, etc., all average out to be $400 a month. Your 30 % is $1,050, and you spend $507 a month, leaving you with $543 to spare. Finally, we get to the last 20 %. This means you have $700 to spend on your remaining 20 %. You can distribute it how you want to when it comes to debt payment and future planning. Since you have the credit card to pay off, you can pay it off within ten months, save $200 every month, so the other $200 can go into your retirement funds, and the final $200 will go into your emergency funds.

The last $100 is for your student loans, and now, if we include the previous 10 % of your income, you can spend it on whatever you want, such as traveling or buying things, whatever you want. If you remember, we had a surplus of $743 a month. Since you now have $743 to spare, what should you do with it? Well, to answer this question, we need to figure out what your overall goals are in life. For example, your main goal this year is to travel to Alaska and to redo your kitchen. Your trip will cost you $500, and your kitchen will cost you around $5,000. What you can do is save $500 of that $743 a month to have the money saved up for the kitchen and also keep the remaining for your trip.

You will have excellently utilized the money, therefore causing you to enjoy your payment and to be smart about it. When you are doing your budget, make sure you are utilizing all these tools to get the best results possible, and to figure out what is important to you. If you have a surplus of money, you can either save it, or you can figure out if there is a more prominent use of that surplus. Some people even donate money to a great cause. So, if that is something you enjoy or would like to take part in, by all means, do that. Overall, do not let the surplus go to waste. Use it for things that have high value to you.

We have pretty much covered up how to use the 50/30/20 rule, so let us give you more reasons as to why you should budget. Look, it does not matter which budget you use, as long as it works for you. If you do not have a budget, you will end up realizing that there are a lot of things that will go wrong, so let us talk about them. The first one does not have a budget. Having a budget is the single most excellent tool that you have to capture everything in your finances. To reach your financial goal, you need a budget; it is easy to get started with it by using the 50/30/20 method or any other method, and it will be useful for your entire life. If you do not have a budget, you need to start one immediately.

If you do not have a budget, it does not mean that you are missing out on being able to use a budget to reach your goal. It is hard, if not impossible, to get a handle on what you are spending your money on or how you are supposed to be saving. If you are on the right track for saving, all of those things can be boiled down to you living a financially free life, so get your budget as soon as possible. Also, estimate your expenses on your budget. The reason that this is so crucial is that most people tend to be bad at remembering how much things cost and what their overall expenses are. Chances are, you do not know your numbers either, which is why it is essential to have your names written.

It is going to be an inadequate budget in the end, and you want your budget to be as accurate as possible. There could be one month where you put less gas, and on the other months, you put more gas, which is why you need to update that number. Also, you need to have something, like supporting documentation. For example, if you forget your numbers, the next month will become a haze for you because of unusual expenses.

This gets us to the point of preparing for the things that pop up, maybe every quarter or every year. These are things that you are not always thinking about; they also add up. Some bills appear quite randomly. Think about things like your car insurance if you are paying that every six months or maybe your car registration, which is happening every year. Even if you are spending your homeowner's insurance every year, you do not have a mortgage, so you are just writing a check for that. These things add up. Also, Christmas and birthdays are kinds of things that are easy to overlook, and some of them can be quite expensive, so you want to incorporate saving for these one-time expenses spread out over a year if it is costly.

Another tip would be that every single budget should have some amount of savings. If you are starting with income at the top, subtracting your expenses, do not wait for savings to be at the end with whatever's left. Make savings a priority. But if you leave it in the end, then you are clearly not prioritizing your savings. One organized tip would be to take the money out of your paycheck and put it directly in a savings account without it even touching your regular checking account. Hopefully, your employer can allow you to send that money instantly to that savings account so that it is done, and it is prioritized. You are less likely to use it accidentally or something like that.

Another no-no is not having an emergency fund budget. Having an emergency fund is a fantastic tool that will allow you to monitor and manage your income for unexpected expenses that are crucial. It is the best way to combat problems in the future, and planning to have an emergency fund in your budget would be fantastic.

If you do not incur any emergency, you can put that money into your savings account. Otherwise, remember that injuries or illness can sometimes take months to recover from; a job can be lost. Make sure that your budget is funding that goal if you do not already have that much today. Another thing you should not do is forgetting to budget for entertainment or fun money. We have always included some amount of fun money or entertainment in our budget. Now, depending on where we were in our financial position, it has very much helped us keep up with our savings budget. We have had a lot of room, and we had a lot of fun sometimes. Also, sometimes, we do not have as much room.

It would help if you had some leg room to have more fun. The truth is that you want to like your budget, and let us be serious who hates having entertainment or fun money. Everybody has an interest or has things that they want to do, and if they are free, then that is fantastic. You can do them a lot. Still, if they are not free, which is okay and pretty standard, then you are going to want to have some money in your account to be able to pay for them, and not having them is going to create a budget that you do not want to stick with.

Finally, you should always be realistic about your spending habits. If this is your first budget or you are updating your budget, then you probably have some big goals, you want to pay off a bunch of debt, or you want to fill that retirement fund. You are prioritizing your emergency and retirement, for example. But you do not want to prioritize them so much that you are unrealistic with how much you are going to spend on your other needs, such as groceries or gas for your car or your car insurance. You will give up on your budgeting if you are too strict with it, which can happen if you try to be too aggressive with cutting your budget. If your budget is aggressively done, it is going to lead to the kind of budget that you will be breaking continually.

With that being said, we conclude this topic. You have to realize that budgeting takes time and effort, and therefore, you need to figure out everything about it before you start working on it. The common misconception is that the 50/30/20 rule is the way to go. But in reality, any budgeting works, as long as it works for you.

This is why we broke down all the mistakes you might be making when you are budgeting. This will give you a better idea of how to budget on your own. Like we mentioned previously if you do not want to follow the 50/30/20 method, that is fine. You can follow any other way that you want.

Trends to Watch Out For

Before we end, here is a quick read about the trends on Instagram that you need to watch out for you to use to your advantage. As Instagram is now going into its ninth year in business, it has evolved throughout the years as new features are continually made available, and people begin incorporating those new features into their user experiences. In the coming years, it is expected that the evolution will continue as we learn how to use these features in new ways to offer unique brand experiences for our audience. Naturally, you do not want to enter a new year using outdated strategies to attempt to target your audience. So, before we begin looking into specific strategies and approaches, we are going to dig into some specific marketing trends and strategies that you will need to look out for. Of course, it is challenging to predict exactly what will come in the new year. We cannot guarantee as to what new features may become available and how updates to the app may change the way we use it when it comes to interacting with your audience.

However, it is pretty clear that specific trends are already growing in popularity, and it is not incredibly challenging to keep track of upcoming trends as long as you learn how to stay engaged. Like any platform, Instagram is filled with patterns that you can quickly identify as long as you are paying attention and engaging with the app regularly. While trends can be hard to predict, there are five trends that we suspect will rise on the Instagram platform in the coming years. The first trend is IGTV, which was launched in June of 2018, but we expect to see it take off and grow even more significant in the next two years. This platform is dedicated to those who use Instagram on their mobile devices and allow individuals to follow YouTube-like channels through the Instagram platform. Unlike other video services, however, IGTV is dedicated to vertical video formatting, which makes it perfect for use on mobile devices, as it offers the ability to watch the videos maximized on your screen. Individuals who are seeking to expand among their mobile audience and start creating more content for their followers to pay attention to can leverage IGTV for a variety of different uses. This includes sharing pieces of wisdom or knowledge in your niche, as well as sharing how-to videos and tutorials.

There are many ways that IGTV can be used to generate sales, but the best way is to ultimately get in front of your audience and start talking about your brand and the ways that you can support your audience through either your products or services.

The key here, however, is to refrain from making it all sound too **salesy**. Instead of talking for five minutes about your service, for example, spend that time building knowledge and offering tips that relate to your audience's problems or challenges and then propose your product or service as a solution. This way, your audience has a valid reason to stay around and listen, rather than making it feel as if you have provided them with a prolonged advertisement for them to watch.

Another trend to keep track of will be the rise of micro-brands, or small businesses, who are sharing their content to followers and getting connected with their audiences. In the past, Instagram has continued to evolve to shine spotlights on small business owners, entrepreneurs, and local brands. It is believed that in the following years, this trend will continue to rise and will make it even easier for micro-brands to connect with their audiences and create an extra income stream through Instagram marketing. The biggest reason that this is likely expanding in trends is that Instagram offers many different ways to share your brand with your audience intimately, and people like sharing that personal connection with the brands they support. Most larger brands do not have the time or the means to offer that intimate relationship with their audience, which is the reason that people are increasingly leaning toward following micro-brands. As a small business owner or a personal brand yourself, having the spotlight being shined primarily on brands just like yours means that now is the perfect time to get on Instagram and start building relationships with customers who are looking for exactly what you offer!

Another trend to continue on Instagram is the use of story advertisements. If you are already on Instagram, you may see sponsored ads rising between the stories that you are watching. These paid advertisements are an opportunity to share screen time with your audience so that they can find your brand and begin following you in the online space. However, you do not have to use paid advertisements to get your advertising in the story feature! The number of templates for story layouts is increasing, which means that you can use the story feature to generate advertisements and share them with your regular story. While these will not go as far and can only be seen by your existing audience or those who locate you and choose to watch your stories, they can still be an excellent opportunity to leverage your stories for advertisement purposes.

Another trend that will continue is one for the e-commerce shops. Here, businesses have the opportunity to begin integrating e-commerce-related features into your page, which makes it easier for customers to locate you and to shop through you.

The most noteworthy feature that offers this right now would be shoppable posts, which allow you to post static images with products in them and then tag the products so that customers can be taken directly to a checkout link. That way, you can post something and encourage people to shop with you through the product tags on your posts. A great example of people doing this would be those who sell clothing or accessories, sharing images featuring their products, and then saying "shop the look!" so that people pause and look at the image. If they like it, they can easily tap the tags on the post and start shopping for the products that they desire. These posts do require a Facebook page integration feature to work, but once you set it up, this feature is incredible, and it is expected that it will evolve to be even more interactive in the coming months.

The fifth trend is one that happens every year in social media and is expected to continue this year: Instagram will be looking for ways to increase engagement with their audience so that their audience spends more time on Instagram. For Instagram, the more popular their platform is, the more people are likely to use it to build their brands and sell their products, which means that Instagram stands to have more paid advertisements going through its platform.

This means that they want to drive as much traffic to the platform as possible, making it even more enjoyable for everyone on the platform. It also means that they keep brands and customers connecting on the platform so that they can continue making money. In other words, Instagram wins when they help small businesses succeed, too, which means that Instagram will continue creating features to help out brands just like yours so that they can continue to grow also.

Conclusion

When you are using Instagram and you are trying to turn your followers into dollars then you know that there are steps you will need to take to make this happen. Followers are an important part of Instagram but another important part of this is realizing how to use them to your benefit. In today's society, everyone is looking for extra income and it is becoming a necessity to do so. As such, people have been learning new ways to find extra income and Instagram is a wonderful way to do this but it takes some work. However, there are many different ways that you can get a lot of benefits and income from this platform.

The first thing that you should remember when you have your followers is to remember that if you build a relationship with your audience because this is going to convert your followers into dollars, which is what we are trying to do here. You should make sure that you are doing your research and see what it is your followers like and what they need. This may sound like something that you would not need but it is and this is important because it lets you develop a personal relationship with your followers. This lets them feel a personal bond or connection with you and this helps them feel closer to you. When they do this, they want to follow you because they feel like they know you. This also helps you understand their needs and what you can do to make them want to stay with you on your account.

This is an important thing for you to understand because it is important to gain followers but it is just as important to be able to keep them. It is great to be able to gain them because that is the first step but if you cannot keep them, you will not be able to turn it into money. This is going to be a problem for you because you are trying to make your Instagram a moneymaker for you as well.

Being loyal is another part of this. Post often. This is a big part of this as well. If you are unable to post every day this is understandable because life happens and emergencies happen as well. If you can try to make it at least once a week with your posts. Your followers will know that you do this and they will look for you and wait to see you. If you need time away simply, let them know and tell them you cannot wait to get back online. This shows them that they have a connection with you and that you are acknowledging it and respecting it at the same time.

Another way to let your followers know they matter? Show you care. Comment back to them and show them that you are taking the time to read what they have to say and that you care about them. This lets them feel more personal with you. Like a friend instead of just some random person on the internet. If you are able to show them that you care about them in a genuine sense, not someone who is pretending, you will find that they will stay with you and not leave for another account.

Everyone likes deals and they love to feel special as well. Many Instagram accounts are popular because they make their followers feel special and being able to offer exclusive deals for those same followers will keep them coming back repeatedly and this has been proven in many different accounts across social media. You still do not have to be complicated. In fact, if you keep them simple and fun it is a lot easier for them and it is a lot easier for you. For example, there are many book authors on Instagram that offers a free copy of their book, exclusive specials that go with their books such as a pin or a signed page, or even a personalized note from the author and all they have to do is follow directions. All they have to do in most cases is follow the account holding the giveaway and leave a comment below and then tag your friends and they get thousands of new followers and thousands of people trying to scramble to get their free item. This is a very good way to gain new people on your account. You could start a deal and keep your followers coming back the same way.

You can also treat your followers with a little special attention. For instance, if you are doing a live chat, you could invite all of your followers to live chat with you and answer questions for them. Let them know that it will be over within a certain amount of time and then you have created a situation where they get to actually talk to you and feel closer to you. This means that they feel like they matter to you and that they're important to you but it also shows that you care about your followers and that you're doing everything you can to make sure that they are staying with you. You are showing loyalty to them and then they, in turn, will show loyalty to you.

Everyone loves to feel special and this is why sending a personalized note or a personalized message is so important. Try not to just say something like I'm excited that you're doing this or this, instead say something like that appeals to them and something that would connect more with them to show that you were paying attention to what they care about and what they need. It can be tempting to promote your business in every post but you cannot stop engaging and providing good content for your followers. Make sure that you have a healthy balance between the two and make sure that you are not doing one over the other so that it does not get too overwhelming or annoying for your fans. This is important because if you are promoting your business more than anything else, chances are your fans are going to get annoyed and you might end up actually losing followers, but if you have a healthy balance between the two, they'll stay interested and they will keep with you.

Promote your followers as well. This is a great way to give back and gain credibility. Pick a day of the week if you choose to and pick a follower that you engage with and then share why you find them so amazing. You could even take it a step further and be the first to comment on why they are a fan of the week and how connecting with fans can be beneficial to the rest of your followers. Share your expertise with them and let them know that you know what you are talking about.

Testimonials are really big and you should take note of the positive things that your clients and customers are saying about you. You can take a huge sense of knowledge from what they are saying. Pay attention to what your followers are saying that they love about you. Sharing testimonials and understanding what it is that your followers love about you remind you of what you can offer them. More than that though, it provides them with the knowledge that they like you for a specific reason and you for that same reason meaning that you are learning the content they want to see because it is what they like about you. It is so much easier to gain followers once you figure out why it is the following you in the first place.

Another great tip that you can take advantage of is value. This ties into everything we have said above because the value is going to help that connection and how people see what you are all about. You should also know what sets you apart from the others in the same field you are in. Let us use the example of you using your Instagram for health and fitness. This is an amazingly popular niche on this app. Therefore, it could be easy for you to get lost among the crowd. You need to avoid this. What sets you apart from the others in that same category? This is something that you need to know because when you do, you convey it to your followers. Then they will see what makes you different. Another tip that can help with this is to know that you can add some value to your bio as well. Tell the people flocking to your page why they should be flocking to you and then following you.

When you post your content, remember your selling proposition. This means the one idea that makes you different and when you are posting to your account, you should be remembering to post your content around that idea. You have value in your content, you deserve to have people see it, and you deserve to make money off it. Share your account with the world and let them see that amazing content.

If you decide to use ads remember to make those about your followers or your audience but not to make them about you. Remember that you need to focus on what they need. Most brands that are out there focus on their own needs instead of the needs of the client. The important thing is that you need to remember that you will need to focus your attention on them and their needs.

Being able to focus on that idea around what you are trying to sell or what you are trying to show the people that are following you is going to help you let them understand that you are talking to them but you are not just trying to sell them things. You are trying to establish a relationship with them that will last. You can also ask questions and have conversations that revolve around the big idea that you have for your profile and your account. Build that trust and let them know that you are looking for relationships not sales. You will be able to get sales later but remember in the beginning you are just trying to get people to follow you.

If you like being controversial, you can be controversial. The most successful brands out there right now have fans as well as big people behind them. Your goal for your posts is to track your prospects and do not stay with everybody else that you do not want. Remember also, you need to be authentic as well. Stop trying to be someone that you are not and instead be real with your audience. You can be different. Different is a great way to stand out. It will let people relate more to people. This because they believe that you are authentic. Being real with your fans could be something as simple as letting them in a little bit on your life. People want to do business with people they know and trust. People want to follow people they know and trust as well.

You also need to focus on the transformation. This is an important part of this and you need to remember it. Your competitors are always focusing on their products and what they can offer people. If you are more advanced than they are, people are going to focus on your benefits and not theirs instead. You need to be advanced and focus on how these benefits are going to impact the lives of the people that are following you. They want to know how working with you or following you is going to be exactly what they are looking for to make them happy and they will want to stay with you and not another person that cannot do that.

When you are on social media, you need to remember that we live in a society that loves and is in love with Instagram. People want to see a clear benefit. They do not buy a product or service; they also buy experience and customer service. They are not just buying what you can do but they are buying how you can help them and treat them. If you do not take the time to share one piece of content that expresses your benefit then you are competition is more than likely to win the battle instead of you. You need to use your social media to articulate your solution and experience that you are going to be using with your audience. You are going to be offering them benefits that other companies cannot and a great way to do this is to remember that you can share stories about past customers and how you were able to help them. This, in turn, would allow the new customers to identify with how you benefit them and know how you are going to benefit them in the future. You can also use social media to articulate what it is that you offer people. For example, if you own a pet store, they are not just coming in to buy dog food, because they can get that anywhere. It is not just food that they are looking for they need to know how your store can benefit them in ways that other people cannot.

Bad habits are horrible and they could end up ruining your chances to be successful. A good example is procrastination. If you find yourself scrolling through Facebook, Twitter or other places like that or if you watch television and you're finding that you're getting too caught up, plan twenty minutes and name a specific time block at the end of your day as well and you'll be able to monitor your social media and respond to questions and engage in situations with the people so that they know that you're fully engaged.

You also need to evaluate your sales process. Is your content proactive or reactive? To make it productive and proactive make sure that your sales are flowing. You are going to need a calendar and map out your content ahead of time so that it will help you stay organized and on track throughout your workday. Most importantly, it is going to keep those people engaged by preventing your content from getting stagnant.

Remember who it is you are writing for. If somebody asked you whom you are writing, for what would you say? You need to do homework by reaching out to your current followers and asking them what it is that they like to see but you can ask those questions about themselves as well so that they need to answer them for you. This is going to let them give you the information that you need and it will help you understand if there is something that you are doing that they do not want to see. If there's something that you're doing that they do want to see more of, being engaged with your audience is the best way to understand what it is that they're looking for because all you have to do is ask them and listen to what they tell you.

You should start looking at data. If you look, at it on your social media networks, it would be able to tell what quality brands are or the data that you need to know to get yours where it needs to be. Data was not created because numbers are pretty. In fact, it is the opposite. It is there to help you understand if you are falling behind or if you need to be working harder. If you want to increase the number of people that are following you and watching you through social media, then you need to dig into those analytics. Data provides brutal facts and you can make good decisions when you understand how to work with that data. The information can be adjusted to suit you better and you can work on your content strategy and how you are positioning the content that you are posting on your Instagram as well as the timing and the length of your posts. All of these things are going to make that data tip in the positive for you instead of in the negative for you. Most importantly, the tips and tricks that we have listed here are going to be able to help you gain followers, keep all the followers that you need and make sure that you are turning them into dollars. This will ensure that you are more successful with your endeavors on Instagram.

Instagram has not failed to show us how visuals can offer brands value to date. The platform has granted many businesses and marketers a platform to make money while portraying themselves as leaders in their field.

The good news is that you can be one of them, and if you properly utilize what Instagram has to offer you, the possibilities are endless. However, if you have no experience using the platform, you will need to put in some effort to ensure you stand out from the others.

I have included lots of helpful information that you can read through, understand,

and implement to ensure you have a seamless Instagram marketing journey.

So why wait? Take the first step now and grow your business and your profits!